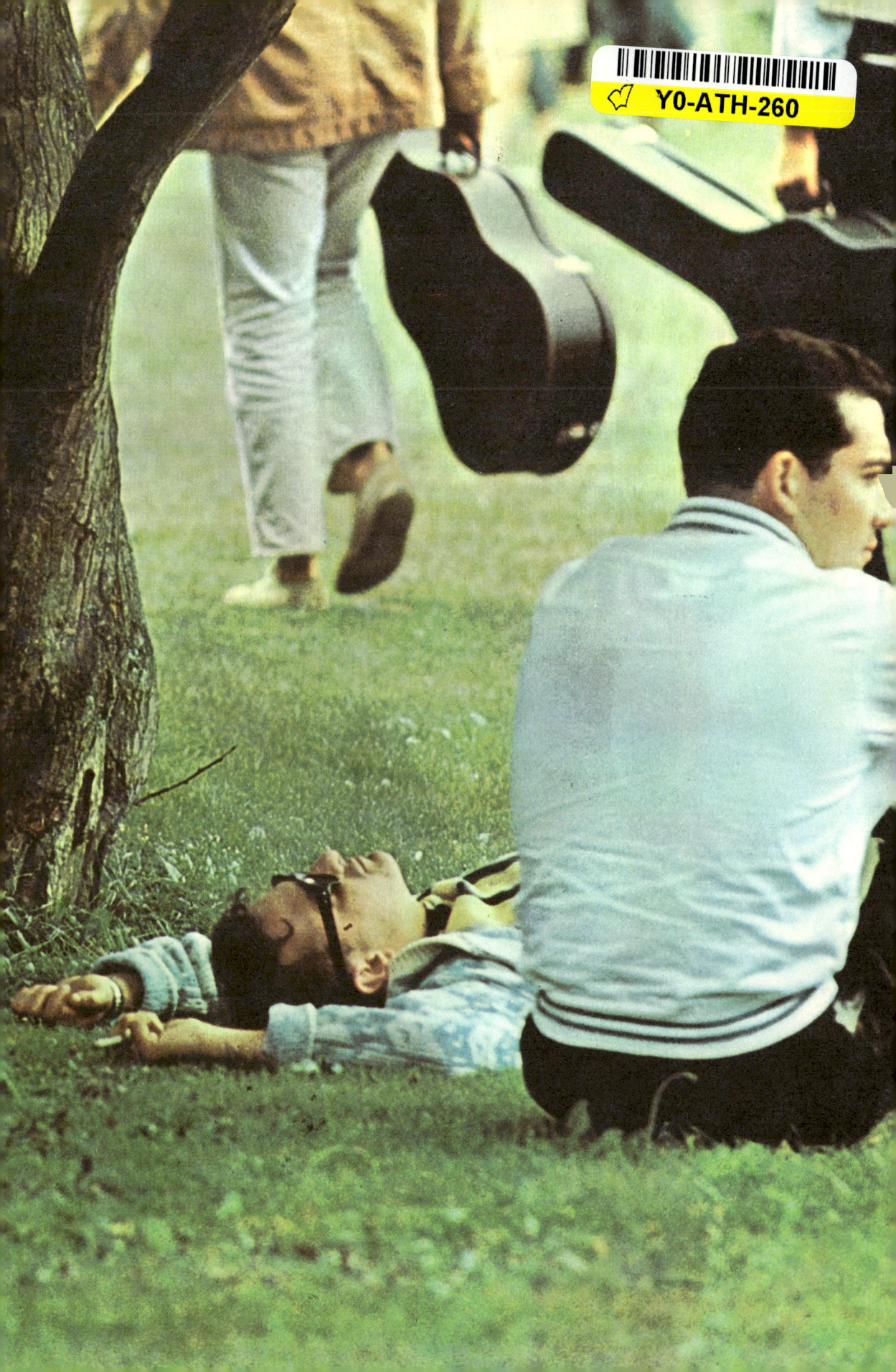

AMERICAN HERITAGE
NEW PICTORIAL
ENCYCLOPEDIC
GUIDE TO THE
UNITED STATES

CREATED AND DESIGNED BY THE EDITORS OF
AMERICAN HERITAGE MAGAZINE

VOLUME

12

PENNSYLVANIA
RHODE ISLAND
SOUTH CAROLINA

PUBLISHED BY
DELL PUBLISHING CO., INC., N.Y.

COMPLETE CONTENTS
OF SIXTEEN VOLUMES

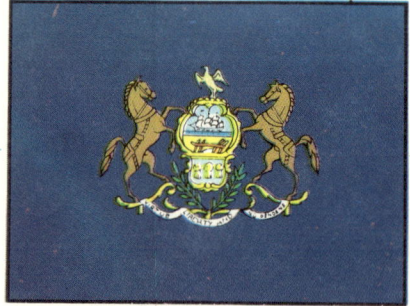

PENNSYLVANIA

RHODE ISLAND

SOUTH CAROLINA

CONTENTS OF VOLUME 12

Front cover: Newport to Bermuda race, Rhode Island Development Council; Wrought-iron gate, Boone Hall, near Charleston, Bruce Roberts, Rapho-Guillumette; Children walking on the Grand Strand, South Carolina State Development Board; Scenic view near Galeton, Pennsylvania, Grant Heilman. Back cover: Providence, Rhode Island, John Lewis Stage; Strasburg Railroad, Pennsylvania, Jim E. Hess; Face of fisherman, Rhode Island, Tony Ray-Jones; Molten iron, Pennsylvania, U.S. Steel Photo; Raven's Cliff Falls, South Carolina, Marlin Spike Werner; Newport Jazz Festival, Rhode Island, Tony Ray-Jones; Narragansett Beach, Rhode Island Development Council; Azaleas, South Carolina, Eugene B. and Kathleen Lewis Sloan; American egret, Rhode Island, John Lewis Stage. Front end sheet: Newport Folk Festival, Rhode Island, Tony Ray-Jones. Back end sheet: Celebration at Southern 500 stock car race, Darlington, South Carolina, Bruce Roberts, Rapho-Guillumette. Flags: Courtesy of Frederick Warne, Ltd., London.

PENNSYLVANIA

Pennsylvania, the Keystone State, which connected the six Northern Colonies with the six in the South, is today an industrial giant: headquarters for the steel and aluminum industries; birthplace of the oil industry; and leading producer of such varied items as shoes, pretzels, and chocolate products. At the same time, it is an important agricultural center, with some of the most fertile and productive farms in America.

Thanks to an early history of religious liberty, Colonial Pennsylvania attracted a wide selection of the world's nationalities and faiths. The mines and factories brought millions of additional immigrants (including, perhaps, the ancestors of the Pittsburgh miner seen on the opposite page). With them came a rich store of skills, beliefs, and traditions.

Pennsylvania's history—as a frontier, as a battleground (in the French and Indian, Revolutionary, and Civil wars), as a granary, as a leader in education, and as a spawner of industries—has paralleled that of the nation. Today, as in the past, the state moves with the national tide. Its eastern and western anchors, Philadelphia and Pittsburgh—and hundreds of cities and towns between—are struggling, sometimes with remarkable success, with urban renewal, conservation of natural resources, civil rights, improved transportation, and all the other pressing problems that engage the citizens of the United States in the second half of the 20th century.

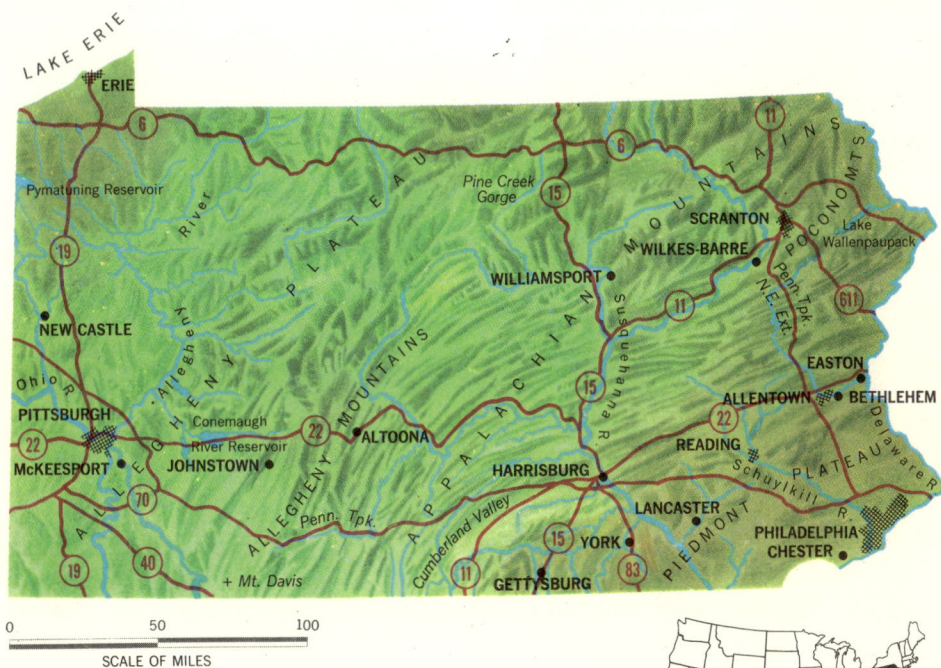

SCALE OF MILES
0   50   100

HALLOWED GROUND

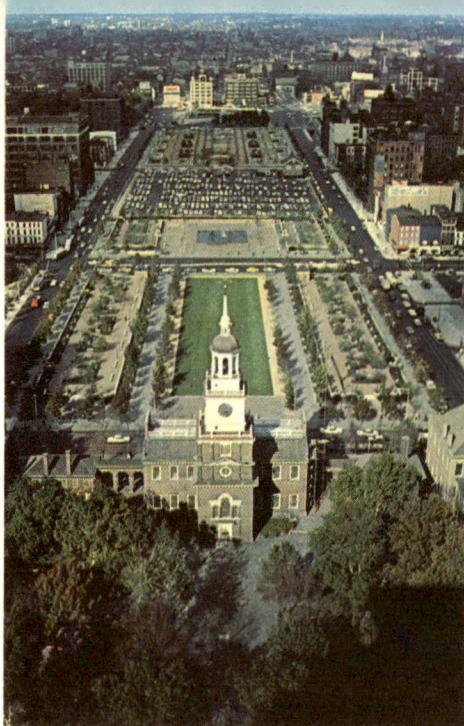
Independence Hall and Mall in Philadelphia

William Penn first sailed up the Delaware River in October, 1682. With him he brought the memory of three imprisonments in England for his Quaker beliefs, the hope of a successful "holy experiment" in the New World, and—more tangibly—a royal grant from Charles II for more than 28 million acres of land, accepted in payment of a debt owed to his father, for whom he named the new land Pennsylvania (Penn's Woods).

Penn quickly opened the colony to thousands of his fellow Quakers, who joined the few hundred settlers already there. Under his leadership, the Great Law of Pennsylvania was framed, giving the franchise to male property owners, providing for the instruction of children, and requiring trial by jury in matters involving life, liberty, and property. Penn dealt justly and peaceably with the Indians. He planned and named the city of Philadelphia.

When the British decided to challenge the French encroachment in the valley of the Ohio River, the western end of the present state became the historical focal point. A 21-year-old colonel, George Washington, suffered a bruising loss at Fort Necessity, and General Edward Braddock blundered into defeat in the Battle of the Wilderness, but the French and Indian War culminated in victory for the British with the fall of Fort Duquesne and the subsequent taking of Quebec. The Treaty of Paris, signed in 1763, ended the French hold on the continent.

By the time of the American Revolution, Pennsylvania had achieved a population of almost 300,000 and a status that was to justify its later designation as the Keystone State, linking the Northern and Southern states of the new Union. The First and Second Continental Congresses met in Philadelphia, whose Independence Hall witnessed the signing of the Declaration of Independence, the adoption of the Articles of Confederation and Perpetual Union, and the framing of the Constitution of the United States. Here, too, Washington accepted command of the Continental Army.

Pennsylvania played a key role in the war against the mother country. Its farmers fed the Revolutionary troops, and its miners and ironworkers provided them with cannons and rifles. Its financiers opened hearts and purses to the effort. Its troops saw action on many fronts. After the American victory at Saratoga, much of the fighting shifted onto Pennsylvania soil—to Brandywine, Paoli, Fort Mifflin, and Germantown. One of the greatest victories of the war—against brute nature and despair, rather than against enemy forces—took place at Valley Forge, where Washington and his ragged troops survived the bitter winter of 1777–78. Nine years later, in 1787, Pennsylvania became the second state to ratify the Constitution, following Delaware by five days.

Washington's headquarters at Valley Forge

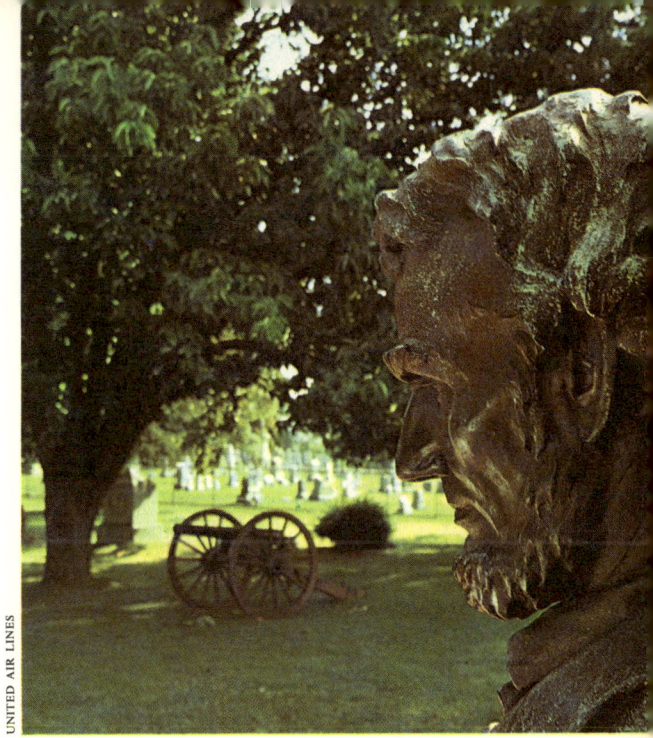

A statue of Abraham Lincoln at Gettysburg

The postwar years saw settlers moving westward in increasing numbers. When western Pennsylvania farmers took arms to oppose an excise tax on distilled liquors, President Washington dispatched a force of 15,000 men. "The Whisky Rebellion," easily suppressed, permitted the young republic to assert itself vigorously in the first major test of federal versus states' rights, an issue still in dispute.

Pennsylvanians then turned their attention to the growth of the state. They built roads, canals, and railroads. They probed the earth for coal, iron ore, and limestone. They constructed mills and factories, forges and foundries. By the eve of the Civil War, the state had become the industrial hearth of the Union.

The Confederate leaders had good reason to look upon Pennsylvania with envy and hatred. Edwin M. Stanton, Union Secretary of War, was a Pittsburgher. The Underground Railroad had flourished in the state. Most important, Pennsylvania was supplying half the Union's steel and four fifths of its military equipment.

It was against this background that Lee made his decision to move north. The climax came at Gettysburg, in what has been ranked as one of the ten most decisive battles in human history. The fighting lasted for three days, July 1–3, 1863. Lee retired from the battlefield on July 4, having lost 28,000 men (killed, wounded, or captured). The North had lost 23,000 men—but had turned the tide of Southern resistance.

The century that followed Gettysburg saw Pennsylvania involved in the great movements that swept across the nation: the growth of industry, the waves of immigration, the problems of urbanization, the burgeoning of technology, the nightmares of world war, and the birth of the atomic age.

But Pennsylvania remains faithful to its memories. The State Historical and Museum Commission administers two museums and 23 historical sites. Independence Hall, with its famed Liberty Bell, is open to the public. Valley Forge State Park contains Washington's headquarters and a museum of battlefield relics. And Gettysburg National Military Park offers guided tours of the battlefield and a dioramic recreation of the three-day battle.

CITY OF BROTHERLY LOVE

Leary's Book Store, the 125-year-old bibliophiles' Eden, has moved the paperbacks up out of its basement to the main floor. The street named for Benjamin Franklin teems with Puerto Ricans. Three apartment towers designed by a Canton-born architect dominate the skyline of Society Hill.

Like many another American city, Philadelphia is boiling with change. Typically, though, the City of Brotherly Love has added some touches of its own.

The "greene countrie towne" was laid out by William Penn (in 1682) in the form of a grid where the Schuylkill and Delaware rivers curve toward each other. After Penn, the city's most illustrious citizen was Franklin, who, although born in Boston, strode up Philadelphia's High Street one Sunday morning in 1723 and went on to make his mark on both Pennsylvania and the nation.

Philadelphia became the nerve center of the Revolution and, from 1790 to 1800, was the Federal Capital. But Franklin would surely be impressed by today's Philadelphia, the fourth most populous city in the nation, a major port, and the scene of a giant renewal program involving 75 separate projects.

One of these has attracted world-wide attention. In what Marshall B. Davidson, the historian, has called "the largest single space available at the center of an American city in the twentieth century," the unsightly "Chinese Wall" of the Broad Street Station and its elevated tracks have given way to the 120-million-dollar complex of handsome office buildings, restaurants, shops, and gardens that is known as Penn Center.

There is more to come. In November, 1964, the city's voters overwhelmingly approved a 162-million-dollar bond issue for such projects as a new stadium in South Philadelphia and improvements in port, library, health, convention, recreation, and transportation facilities.

In its rebuilding the city has remembered its historic past. Independence Hall, the nation's birthplace, has been freed of the surrounding loft buildings that once hid it from view. Carpenter's Hall, which once rang to the voice of Patrick Henry, has been similarly liberated. The old homes of Society Hill have been rescued from their

Above: Students at Swarthmore. Right: An aerial view of Philadelphia, with City Hall in the foreground. Below: The annual Mummer's Parade.

dreary role as boardinghouses. Elfreth's Alley has been preserved much as it was in Colonial times. The 4,076-acre oasis of Fairmount Park displays 23 historic homes, six open to the public.

One of the city's chief problems has been its racial upheaval. The first Negroes came as slaves; others followed when Philadelphia gained fame as an antislavery center. During World War II, thousands migrated from the South to seek jobs in industry. This influx, coupled with a white exodus, has given the Negro—with more than one fourth of the city's population—the balance of political power. Officials predict that by 1980 Negroes will make up 40 per cent of the city's population. Philadelphia's leaders have been working to improve the lot of nonwhite citizens, and significant gains have been made in the areas of housing, income, and education. The problem is still a pressing one, however, and is likely to remain so for many years to come.

The waves of change have battered even the Main Line, a 17-mile-long strip of townships to the west. Developed by the Pennsylvania Railroad less than a century ago, the Main Line became known for its great estates, resort hotels, and horse- and beagle-loving aristocracy. After World War I it developed a solid, permanent population, but kept its reputation for exclusiveness. Today, though, there are sizable Negro communities in Ardmore and Bryn Mawr (site of an excellent women's college), and other newcomers are at least tolerated, perhaps as replacements for the estimated 30 per cent of the Main Line's young people who are at present moving out.

The Main Line remains, but, as James Michener points out, its "suburban life is good only so long as the parent city is strong and vital." Philadelphia offers its splendid Museum of Art and Franklin Institute; its great symphony orchestra; the educational institutions—Pennsylvania, Temple, and Villanova universities, La Salle, St. Joseph's, and Swarthmore colleges, Drexel Institute of Technology —that fill and ring the city; and so many rich sights that, as an article in the *New York Times* said, walking anywhere in the city "is like picking up the Bible or Shakespeare and reading at random."

SKYPHOTOS, PHILADELPHIA

999

Left: A view of the Delaware River, between Easton and New Hope. Above: Three of the busy piers on Philadelphia's water front. Below: An aerial view of Levittown, a huge housing development.

ALONG THE DELAWARE

The Delaware is the easternmost of Pennsylvania's three leading rivers (the others being the Susquehanna and the Allegheny-Ohio). It rushes out of New York's Catskill Mountains to form a short stretch of that state's border with Pennsylvania. For most of its 296-mile length it draws a meandering line of separation between Pennsylvania and New Jersey. It is fed by the Lehigh and the Schuylkill, capturing more than 14 per cent of the state's drainage. Along its western bank, before the river ends in Delaware Bay, is a varied panorama of farmland, industry, and scenic resorts.

The Delaware touches Pennsylvania in the northeastern dairyland of rural Wayne County. It flows past Pike County, whose beauty and abundance so enthralled Horace Greeley that he founded his Utopian Sylvania Colony there in 1842.

Near Stroudsburg the river puts on its most spectacular show at the Delaware Water Gap, a breath-taking gorge framed by steep slopes covered with the state flower, mountain laurel. West of the gap spread the Pocono Mountains, one of the nation's favorite playgrounds, a land of waterfalls, trout streams, golf courses, hunting grounds, mountain lakes, and ski developments.

The shore takes on the silhouette of industry at Easton, a manufacturing community situated in a rich farming area, and starting point for what was once a continuous system of Indian paths that reached as far as Pittsburgh. A short distance inland stand two of the state's most important manufacturing cities. Allentown is the center of America's leading cement producing district (and annually stages what is one of the largest county fairs in the nation). Bethlehem is noted not only for its great iron and steel plants but also for its reputation as America's

Christmas City—a 100-foot electric star burns brightly atop South Mountain every yuletide—and for its Bach festival, which is held every May.

Bucks County is a singular combination of bucolic pursuit and international influence. Geographer-planner Jean Gottmann has called it the financial and managerial "Main Street of the modern world." One of its townships is home to more than 40 millionaires and a small army of artists, writers, and theatre people.

Bucks County is as various as its many communities. New Hope, named for the gristmill that now is the esteemed Bucks County Playhouse, is famous for its creative colony and for the mule-drawn barges that take sightseers along its canals. Doylestown boasts the vast collection of the Mercer Museum, a display of tools, machines, and manuscripts of the days before steam power. Morrisville combines new and old with its giant Fairless Works and the nearby Pennsbury Manor, a reconstruction of William Penn's country estate; a few miles up the Delaware is Washington Crossing State Park, dedicated to the memory of the 2,400 Revolutionary soldiers who crossed the river on Christmas night to capture Trenton from the Hessians. Levittown, with its thousands of homes laid out in swirling rows, and its tight, self-sufficient master blocks, has been referred to as the most carefully planned city since Major Pierre Charles L'Enfant laid out Washington, D.C.

Just before ending its southward course, the Delaware passes the water front of Philadelphia, the state's leading port area. In recent years the city has improved its warehouse and dock facilities in a bid for more foreign trade; the Delaware River ports, including Philadelphia, now rank first in the U.S. in imports handled and second in total tonnage.

THE PENNSYLVANIA DUTCH

To their new neighbors they were "dumb Dutch." Benjamin Franklin called them "Palatine boors" and asked, "Why should Pennsylvania, founded by the English, become a colony of aliens, who will shortly be so numerous as to Germanize us, instead of our Anglifying them?"

The Pennsylvania Dutch—or Pennsylvania Germans as they are sometimes called—were neither dumb nor boorish. When they arrived late in the 17th century, they were indeed mute, but that condition was attributable to the simple fact that they spoke no English. Their aloofness grew out of the repression and persecution from which they had fled.

Nevertheless, they quickly made their influence felt. In 1688 they produced the first written protest against slaveholding in America. They gave the continent its first symphony orchestra. During the Revolutionary War they cast the cannon that helped turn back the British. Their farms fed Washington's troops. They invented and produced the Conestoga wagon. Their Pennsylvania rifle kept the frontiersmen in game and defended pioneer homes against Indian attack.

The Pennsylvania Dutch have been active in political life. Michael Hillegas, acting for the Continental Congress, was the first Treasurer of the United States. Frederick Augustus Conrad Muhlenberg

A group of Amish farmers attend a sale of farm equipment at Bird-in-Hand in Lancaster County.

JIM E. HESS

served as first Speaker of the U.S. House of Representatives. The Pennsylvania Dutch have provided 10 governors of the commonwealth.

After almost 300 years in America, the Pennsylvania Dutch continue to be the subject of many misconceptions. They are neither "Dutch" nor wholly German, their forebears having been mainly Germans, Swiss, and Alsatians. They are not confined to Pennsylvania, but have migrated in groups as far as California, Canada, and Mexico. The Amish, Mennonites, and other "plain people," known for their beards, black hats, and simple ways, form only a small minority of the Pennsylvania Dutch, while the majority are "church people"—for the most part Lutherans, Reformed, and Moravians.

The Pennsylvania Dutch remain a conspicuous element in the state. The "seven sweets and seven sours" represent an understatement of the groaning boards that distinguish Pennsylvania Dutch cookery, a cuisine ranked with the French Creole of Louisiana as one of America's finest. The great stone barns still stand on the country's most productive farms. The misnamed "hex" signs express a love of color and design that is repeated in painted dower chests, housewares, and illuminated *fraktur* manuscripts, many of which can be seen in the Pennsylvania Farm Museum of Landis Valley, near Lancaster.

For transportation Amish families use horses and buggies, like the one seen in this photograph.

In the 1859 photograph at left Edwin Drake stands by the world's first oil well, at Titusville. Above, Pennsylvania miners at the turn of the century descend a shaft in a rickety cage.

PETROLEUM AND COAL

Pennsylvania's industrial might stems from the state's plentiful hydrocarbon resources. Nature deposited a rich bed of bituminous coal under the soil of the western counties. East of the Susquehanna, lucrative veins of anthracite were laid down. And in the northwest section of the state, oil lay close enough to the surface to yield to the crude drilling devices of the 1850's.

The petroleum industry was born at Titusville. There, in 1859, a retired railroad conductor named Edwin L. Drake drilled the world's first successful oil well. It produced at less than 70 feet, and started a gigantic industry.

By the end of the 19th century, Pennsylvania had yielded its dominant position in oil. (It was Pennsylvania money

that helped to finance the spectacularly successful Spindletop well in Texas.) Nevertheless, the Keystone State still has some 66,000 producing wells in the western region, and almost one fourth of the nation's motor oil comes from Pennsylvania crude oil. Pittsburgh's Gulf Oil Corporation is the world's third largest producer. The area along the Delaware River between Philadelphia and Chester is a great refining and research center.

Coal preceded petroleum as a factor in the state's growth. Anthracite fed the early iron mills, and the Age of Steel produced a near-unquenchable demand for coke made from bituminous coal.

In recent years the industry has come upon hard times. Some of its richest fields have been depleted. Air pollution controls

Modern equipment: the steel-toothed, rotating cutterheads of a continuous mining machine tear coal from the wall and drop it to the floor. Then gathering arms and a conveyer belt pick it up.

and the encroachment of competitive fuels have crowded coal out of the home-heating market. Pennsylvania has passed strict strip mine control legislation. The railroads have adopted diesel engines. Steelmen have learned more efficient ways of using coke, and the utilities have squeezed more kilowatt-hours from every ton of coal. Over the horizon looms the threat—and the promise—of the atom. (The world's first atomic power plant was built in coal country, at Shippingport.)

Pennsylvania continues to supply almost all of America's anthracite needs, but it has fallen to third place in bituminous and second in total coal output.

The industry has worked hard to improve its reputation and its methods. Although employment has dropped drastically, those who remain enjoy working conditions, compensation, and fringe benefits that are a far cry from the time of the company police and the $1.60-a-day pay envelope. Efficiency has been improved to the point where American coal competes successfully in European and Asian markets. Laboratories work to develop new uses for coal. The generating of electricity from mine sites holds new promise. And machinery suppliers continue to provide marvels of mechanization like the new Joy Pushbutton Miner, in which a single operator, comfortably seated in an air-conditioned cab, reads a battery of control instruments as he manipulates a boring head that chews coal a thousand feet inside the earth and returns it to the surface on continuous conveyers.

1005

Above, steel is poured into ingot molds at Bethlehem Steel Company's plant in Johnstown, the city in which 2,200 people were drowned in a flood in 1889. Below, Bethlehem's Pittsburgh plant.

STEEL FOR THE NATION

For almost a century, Pennsylvania has led the states in production of steel. Pennsylvania iron and steel have armed the nation in all its major conflicts. Railroading, the manufacturing of motors and electrical machinery, and thousands of other industries owe their existence to the state's prodigious output of ferrous metals. Pennsylvania today contains almost one third of the country's steel plants and roughly 20 per cent of U.S. steel capacity. It regularly accounts for 20 to 25 per cent of American steel production.

William Penn was one of the first to identify the area's potential. He had owned an ironworks in England and was quick to note the existence of ore deposits in his new colony. Thomas Rutter, a Quaker blacksmith, produced Pennsylvania's first commercial iron in Berks County in 1716. In the 18th century the river valleys in the eastern part of the state were dotted with "iron plantations," surrounded by virgin forests that provided wood for charcoal to be used in the blast furnaces and forges—in many cases, at the rate of an acre of timber a day.

These areas went into decline when wood gave way to coal. Pittsburgh, built in the heart of the bituminous coal region and having access to the ore mines of Lake Superior and other fields, gained an ascendancy in the industry that it still enjoys. Along its rivers now range the great plants of United States Steel Corporation, Jones and Laughlin, and other producers. The city today is the capital of a region that produces more steel than most of the world's nations.

Outside Pittsburgh, the state boasts a number of steel centers. Bethlehem, which is near deposits of anthracite, is the home of Bethlehem Steel Company, which has another large installation at Steelton and has poured $200 million into its Johns-town plant in little more than a dozen years. U.S. Steel built the world's largest continuous-flow steel mill on a 3,900-acre site at Morrisville, where ocean-going freighters could sail up the Delaware to unload Venezuelan and Canadian ore directly at the plant site; the 450-million-dollar Fairless Works, nearby, produces three million tons of steel a year.

The steel industry, recently emerged from a shaky period characterized by increased competition from other materials and other nations, is currently on its way to new records for production and profits. Steelmen have been among the most enthusiastic converts to the technology of automation and computer-run processing lines. An indication of their success is that steel production in Pennsylvania went up by 76.2 per cent in the period from July, 1962, to July, 1964, while employment increased by only 11.3 per cent. According to a United Steelworkers survey, raw steel production has risen to an annual rate of 287 tons per blue collar worker, compared to 240 in 1962.

Steel glories today in a self-promoted revolution in technology. It spends about $100 million a year for research, and has tripled the number of its scientists and engineers since 1952. Three major developments have changed the face of steel. The basic oxygen furnace involves the use of a water-cooled nozzle that blows oxygen at more than 200 cubic feet per second over the surface of a molten charge; the result is better steel made at lower cost and in one fifth to one eighth of the time formerly required. Continuous casting produces slabs that can be sliced and sent directly to the rolling mill, eliminating reheating and a number of other steps. And in vacuum degassing, molten steel is agitated to permit the release of tiny bubbles of hydrogen, nitrogen, and oxygen.

A NEW PITTSBURGH

Pittsburgh's renaissance began with the end of World War II. An air pollution control program was instituted, banning soot-producing home fuels and requiring industry to spend $275 million for smoke-abating equipment. The city that Dickens once called "hell with the lid off" now boasts the cleanest skies in the nation.

Another major step was the removal of the industrial slum along The Point, where the Allegheny and Monongahela rivers meet to form the Ohio. In what is now known as Gateway Center, a modern hotel, an upper-income apartment building, and a complex of office structures rise over broad, tree-lined walks. A short distance away, the headquarters of Aluminum Company of America and United States Steel Corporation, gleaming towers of metal and glass, face each other across the splashing fountains of Mellon Square Park. At the foot of the Hill District, Pittsburgh's Harlem, stands the new Civic Arena, with a retractable dome that is the largest in the world. The new Pittsburgh Center for the Arts will rise nearby.

In all, the city has 17 urban renewal and redevelopment projects under way, many of them aimed at the elimination of residential slums and the relocation of affected families.

The city is conscious that its prosperity was built on steel and coal, followed by aluminum, electrical machinery, and other

heavy industries. Civic forces have now rallied to promote greater diversification. A major talking point has been the area's research community, with an investment of more than $350 million. The Panther Hollow research park, a 250-million-dollar project, will spread over a two-mile-long ravine in the Oakland section.

Pittsburgh enjoys excellent cultural facilities. Its symphony orchestra won acclaim during a 1964 tour of Europe and the Middle East. The triennial Pittsburgh International is one of the outstanding events of the art world. The University of Pittsburgh, Carnegie Institute of Technology, and Duquesne University have a total enrollment of more than 23,000.

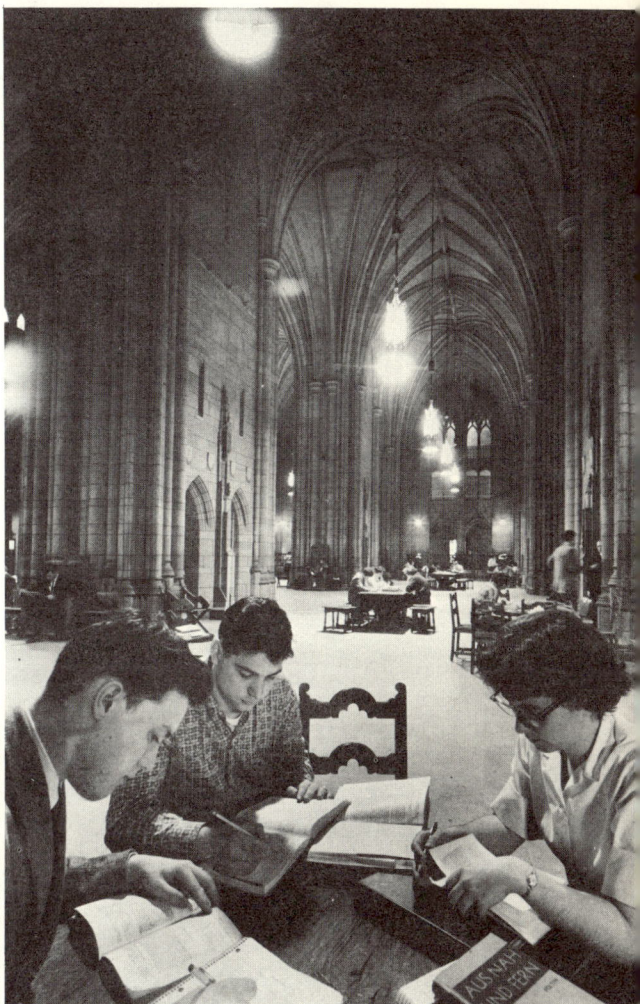

Top: Pittsburgh Auditorium (the dome rolls back in good weather). Above: Students in the common room at the University of Pittsburgh. Left: Pittsburgh's Golden Triangle during the course of the massive modernization program.

PENNSYLVANIA
FLORA AND FAUNA

BIRDS

1) Peregrine Falcon (Mature);
2) Peregrine Falcon (Immature);
3) Common Raven; 4) Ruffed Grouse;
5) Golden-winged Warbler;
6) Solitary Vireo; 7) Cliff Swallow

TREES

1) Eastern Hemlock; 2) Eastern Red Cedar;
3) Chestnut Oak; 4) Scarlet Oak;
5) White Birch; 6) Honey Locust

FLOWERS

1) Mountain Laurel; 2) Large Toothwort;
3) Orange Hawkweed;
4) Small White Lady's-slipper;
5) Hop Clover

ANIMAL LIFE

1) Red Bat; 2) Star-nosed Mole;
3) New England Cottontail;
4) Allegheny Wood Rat;
5) White-tailed Deer;
6) Ribbon Snake; 7) Gray Fox

CHARLES FRACE

"FAST FAT EARTH"

From the time of its first settlement until well into the 19th century, Pennsylvania enjoyed a reputation as "the bread-basket of America." What the geologists call Hagerstown soil, and what William Penn wrote of as "fast fat earth," had already produced the sylvan abundance that gave the state the second part of its name. It remained only for the new farmers to hack clearings in the woods and spread seed in the earth, which is among the richest in the world.

Today, in spite of its emphasis on industry, Pennsylvania remains an important factor in America's agricultural economy. It leads the nation in production of state-graded eggs, state-graded apples, cigar-leaf tobaccos, mushrooms, and plantation-grown Christmas trees. It is second in buckwheat production and value of chickens. It ranks among the top five states in such diverse items as sour cherries, maple syrup, milk, peaches, and grapes. Its 90,000 farms, including buildings, equipment, livestock, and crops, have been valued at more than $4 billion, which is a larger capital investment than that of either mining or manufacturing of primary metals.

As elsewhere in the nation, farm population has been declining while productivity has been going up. Two figures are particularly revealing: Pennsylvania ranks thirty-second among states in farm acreage but fourteenth in the value of its farm products. The figures pay tribute to the efficiency of Pennsylvania farms, which produce, on the average, more wheat per acre than farms in the traditional Wheat Belt states do.

Cash income from the marketing of Pennsylvania's farm production, supplemented by government subsidies, amounts to some $800 million annually. Of this, roughly 70 per cent comes from the sale of livestock, including poultry and eggs.

The state's prime agricultural areas lie in the east, particularly along the Maryland border in Lancaster and York counties, whose prosperous farms testify to the assiduous husbandry of the Pennsylvania Dutch. Lancaster, with more than 4,500 farms, has been called the most diversified agricultural county in the nation, and stands first in value of crops grown without benefit of irrigation. Across the Susquehanna, the neighboring county of York

has 2,700 farms (followed by Bradford in the northeast and Crawford in the northwest, with more than 2,000 farms each). In recent years, the southeastern portion of the state has become important as a grazing center for Western cattle bound for Eastern markets. Adams and Franklin counties, along the south central border, lead in peach and apple production, while the Erie region's vineyards, to the delight of wine lovers, serve the largest grape processing plant in the country.

Above: Tobacco is baled in Lancaster County.
Below: The rich farmlands of York County.

THE PROBLEM OF APPALACHIA

Appalachia has become a symbol of Americans' concern for their less fortunate brethren. The area begins at Pennsylvania's northern border and extends as far south as Alabama. Technically, Pennsylvania's Appalachia embraces 52 of the state's 67 counties, excluding only the southeast. The heart of the region, however, the place where the problems are the greatest, runs through the interior of the state and includes such middle-sized cities as Altoona, Johnstown, Scranton, Wilkes-Barre, and Harrisburg (the capital), and little towns like Shenandoah, whose citizens would hardly fill a metropolitan basketball arena.

Pennsylvania's Appalachian population numbers almost six million. Its unemployment rate, however, is lower than in the rest of Appalachia, its per capita income higher. An editor in one of the hardest-hit towns says: "Nobody is starving here, nobody is deprived of medical care, nobody goes without shelter."

Many of the communities' problems stem from the industries—primarily steel, coal, and railroading—that once gave them prosperity and, in some cases, brought them into being. Coal, in particular, has borne the brunt. Employment in the industry has dropped to one third of what it was in 1947. Surface and underground fires, subsidence, and acid drainage from strip mines have endangered lives, destroyed property, and discouraged industry. The state government has taken heroic measures. It has quenched 27 underground fires since 1953, flushed fill material back into dozens of mines, and passed what it calls the most modern strip mine control legislation in the country.

In the drive to rebuild, the communities

GRANT HEILMAN

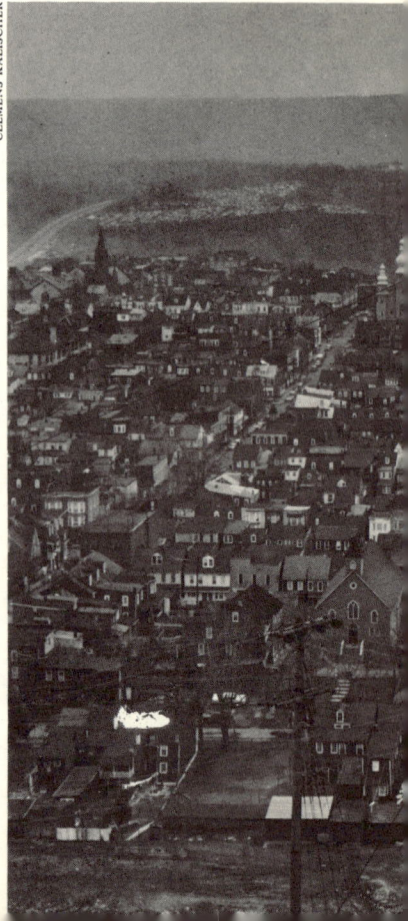

CLEMENS KALISCHER

themselves have led the way. The Scranton Plan for local financing of plant facilities has attracted makers of such products as textiles, electric organs, Geiger counters, and aircraft parts. In Wilkes-Barre, labor and industry have joined with Wilkes College in a program that has created 10,000 new jobs, which in turn have generated 10,000 more. The pattern is repeated throughout the state.

The net migration from Pennsylvania's Appalachia between 1950 and 1960 was more than half a million. Nevertheless, home ties are hard to break. C. W. Dressler, associate editor of the *Johnstown Tribune-Democrat*, says: "If you are going to be poor, there are few better places than this Appalachian region to be poor in. When our people lose or can't find work elsewhere, they tend to come back to the friendly mountains."

ABOVE AND BELOW: CLEMENS KALISCHER

Far left: The State Capitol area in Harrisburg. Left: Shenandoah, a small mining town in eastern Pennsylvania, 11 miles north of Pottsville. Top: Members of the Greek Orthodox Church in Shenandoah. Above: A Shenandoah laborer.

PENNSYLVANIA LEGENDS AND LORE

In *Poor Richard's Almanack*, a farmer's calendar and weather guide, appeared hundreds of aphorisms that delighted Colonial Americans. Produced by Benjamin Franklin, the *Almanack* contained such pithy remarks as:

"The worst wheel on the cart makes the most noise."

"Fish and visitors stink in three days."

"Early to bed and early to rise makes a man healthy, wealthy and wise."

Although Franklin became one of the most distinguished of his country's founders, his wit never flagged. It was Franklin who is supposed, after having heard John Hancock say, "We must all hang together," as he signed the Declaration of Independence, to have wryly replied: "Yes, we must indeed all hang together or most assuredly we shall all hang separately."

Franklin was one of the first American practitioners of the tall tale. Expounding on the wealth of the Colonies, he wrote in a London newspaper that "the very tails of the American sheep are so laden with wooll, that each has a little car or waggon on four little wheels, to support

& keep it from trailing on the ground." Ben also explained the presence of salt water creatures in the Great Lakes by stating: "that cod, like other fish when attacked by their enemies, fly into any water where they can be safest; that whales, when they have a mind to eat cod, pursue them wherever they fly; and that the grand leap of the whale in that chase up the Fall of Niagara is esteemed, by all who have seen it, as one of the finest spectacles in nature."

Perhaps Benjamin Franklin rose so fast in William Penn's colony because he was among people who understood him. Poor Richard's "Many Words won't fill a Bushel," is close in spirit to the Pennsylvania Dutchman's admonition to his hen, "If you cackle, lay." Pennsylvania folklore from Colonial times to the present has received its greatest influence from these German farmers who came from the Palatine to escape the wars and religious persecution of 18th-century Europe. Settling throughout the state they were nicknamed the Pennsylvania Dutch, and their jokes and proverbs were repeated everywhere. "A big wife and a big barn will

never do a man any harm." "When a pig has enough it upsets the trough." "'One must remember where it comes from,' said the farmer when the mule kicked him."

Today, many of these "Dutch" still inhabit the rolling hills of Pennsylvania, preserving the sayings and riddles of their ancestors. What goes and goes, and yet stands and stands? Answer—a mill.

One may hear tales of the trickster Eileschpijjel (or Eilenshpiggel). His master once told him to load up a wagon and he started throwing ears of corn into it. "Well, if the horse can pull this one, he can pull another one!" cried Eileschpijjel as he threw ear after ear of corn into the wagon. When he finally stopped, the wagon was too heavy to pull. "Well, if he can't pull this one, he can't pull that one," muttered Eileschpijjel, and one by one he threw out every ear of corn from the wagon and then drove away with an empty cart.

Another favorite kind of story centers about the pastor—for though the Dutch are a very religious people, they love to joke. "How is the devil today?" a farmer asked sarcastically of one zealous preacher as he met him on the road. The pastor smiled and, taking the man's hand, replied, "It's such a pleasure to find one like you, so concerned for his father's health."

The most striking contributions of the Pennsylvania Dutch to America's folklore have been the Christmas tree and the Easter bunny. Why does the Easter bunny leave eggs? The answer is in an old myth from the days when Germany was a pagan land. It seems that the goddess Ostara, at the request of the rabbit, changed him from a bird into an animal. Before this the rabbit had wings and flew. As a sign of his gratitude to the goddess, the rabbit would lay an egg on Ostara's feast day, each year. When Germany became Christianized, this story became part of the holiday celebration of Easter. Though the goddess Ostara was discarded, the rabbit remained to distribute his eggs. In some Pennsylvania hamlets he leaves them in a basket on the front steps. In others, he hides them in the fields or under tree trunks. In some homes the boys and girls put their caps and bonnets under the kitchen table, and when the Easter bunny arrives, he lays his colored eggs in them.

Forest Scene on the Tobihanna, Allegheny Mountains *(above) is an aquatint made by Karl Bodmer in 1833. Below, automobiles on the Pennsylvania Turnpike pass through Blue Mountain Tunnel.*

TRANSPORTATION LEADER

Pennsylvania has written some of the brightest pages in the history of transportation. The Conestoga wagon, a wide-wheeled "ship of inland commerce" invented by the Pennsylvania Dutch, carried thousands of tons of goods across the state and to the Western frontier. Pennsylvanians built the canals and locks that opened the rivers to year-round passage. They pioneered in railroading and highway construction. The aluminum industry, born in Pittsburgh, helped speed the progress of aviation.

Water has figured prominently in the state's development. Pennsylvania is the only state that enjoys access to the two major Eastern waterways, as well as to the Atlantic Ocean. Pittsburgh is the terminus of the route connecting the Ohio River to the Gulf of Mexico via the Mississippi. Erie opens onto the Great Lakes and the St. Lawrence Seaway. Philadelphia has become a major Atlantic port, with regularly scheduled ship service to more than 100 foreign countries.

In 1829, on a trial run from Carbondale to Honesdale, "the Stourbridge Lion" became America's first steam locomotive to run on rails. Around the same time Pennsylvanians conquered the mountains by building the 37-mile-long Allegheny Portage Railroad, an engineering marvel that raised and lowered canal boats on cable-drawn flat cars up and down 10 inclined planes, passing for 900 feet through what may have been the nation's first railroad tunnel, and terminating in Johnstown.

Railroads have helped shape the state's destiny ever since. Pennsylvania is now served by 14 major trunk lines and 36 smaller terminal lines, running on some 9,500 miles of track. The Pennsylvania Railroad is the largest railroad system in the world.

It is in highways that Pennsylvania has achieved its greatest reputation for transportation progress. More than 100,000 miles of road give the state the largest system of highways in the country, larger than those of New York and the New England states combined. The network's chief artery is the Pennsylvania Turnpike, which pierces the mountains through tunnels built by steel magnate Andrew Carnegie for a proposed railroad. It was opened in 1940 as "the first long distance highway in America . . . without cross traffic at grade anywhere." Serial extensions have stretched the turnpike to its present 359-mile length from the Ohio border to New Jersey. A 110-mile-long northward link takes travelers from Philadelphia to Bethlehem, Wilkes-Barre, and Scranton. A parallel turnpike, the Keystone Shortway, to be completed in the late 1960's, will span the state's center.

A barge on the Delaware Canal near New Hope

BUCKS COUNTY HISTORICAL-TOURIST COMMISSION, SARA M. CLARK

RECREATION

In 1954 a Pennsylvania governor-to-be was asked his plans for increasing tourism. He replied: "Let's face it. This just isn't a tourist state." Ten years later, he could regret his words: tourism was bringing $2 billion a year into the state, second only to manufacturing.

A major stimulant has been Pennsylvania's variety of natural attractions. There are more than 60 state parks, 48 state forest picnic areas, two state forest monuments, and seven natural areas. Some 15 million acres, more than half the state total, lies in woodlands. Man-made lakes and reservoirs augment the abundant water resources of the state.

For the sportsman, Pennsylvania encourages hunting and fishing. With more than six million acres open to hunters, the state leads all others in its annual take of deer and bear. Bear country extends across the northern counties. Deer are more plentiful in the mountains, but larger near farmlands. Small game, found everywhere, includes wild turkey, ring-necked pheasant, woodcock, quail, ruffed grouse, waterfowl, rabbit, and squirrel. For anglers, there are hundreds of species of fish, the most popular being trout, bass, walleyes, northern pike, pickerel, and muskellunge. The Fish Commission annually stocks lakes and streams with millions of legal-sized trout.

Winter sport has become a major industry; no spot in the state lies more than a few hours' drive from one of 33 prime ski areas.

Among the state's scenic treats are Presque Isle State Park, with its seven miles of sandy beach along Lake Erie; the Pocono Mountains; the Delaware Water Gap, slicing between the steep slopes of the Kittatinny Mountains; and the ubiquitous forests and rolling hills that are found throughout the state.

Cook Forest State Park (left) is a peaceful area of pine and hemlock. Top: Pennsylvanians ride to the hounds during the Radnor Hunt Meeting at Willistown. Above is a photograph of Presque Isle State Park, situated near Erie.

PENNSYLVANIA PLACES OF INTEREST

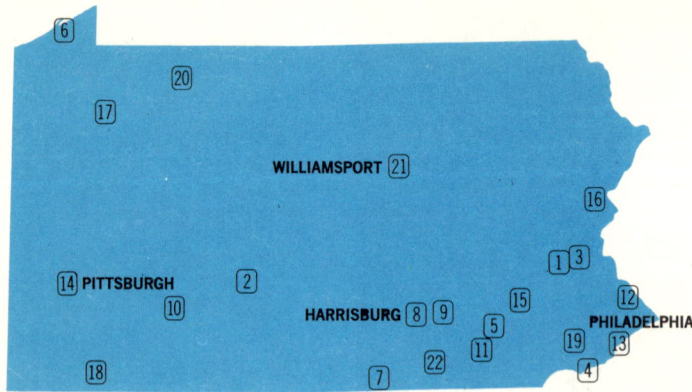

1 ALLENTOWN
When the British advanced on Philadelphia after the Battle of Brandywine in 1777, patriots rushed the Liberty and Christ Church bells to Allentown for safekeeping in the Zion's Reformed Church. The Liberty Bell Shrine in the church that now stands on the site contains a full-sized replica of the original bell. The restored Trout Hall (1770) is now a museum and library.

2 ALTOONA
Founded by the Pennsylvania Railroad in 1849 as a terminal of the first railroad over the Alleghenies, Altoona has the largest railroad shops in the world. The famed Horseshoe Curve, about five miles west of town, can be best seen from an ideally situated parking area reached via Pennsylvania Route 193. The curve, constructed in 1852, sweeps for 2,375 feet through the mountains.

3 BETHLEHEM
When Moravians from Bohemia and Saxony finished building their first community structure, a log cabin, just before Christmas, 1741, they sang songs, including a hymn that gave their town its name. Bethlehem now is famous both for steel and music; it is the site of the parent plant of the Bethlehem Steel Corporation, and a Bach festival is held every May. At Christmas a 100-foot-tall electric star shines from the top of South Mountain and traditional Moravian carols are sung along with the music of Mozart and Handel. Moravian buildings include the Gemein Haus (1742); the adjoining Old Chapel (1751); the Bell House (1746); Main Hall Museum; and the Brethren's House (1748), which became America's first museum in 1763. The historic section of old Bethlehem is being restored.

4 CHESTER
This busy Delaware River port and shipbuilding center, founded by Swedes in 1644 as Upland, is the state's oldest existing town. Visitors may tour the Sun Shipbuilding and Dry Dock Company. A marker indicates the site of the Essex House, where William Penn spent his first night on American soil. Also noteworthy are the Colonial Courthouse (1724), the oldest public building in the state, and, several miles away, the Caleb Pusey House (1683), the oldest house in the state. About two miles northeast, near Essington, is Governor Printz Park, site of the state's first settlement. The John Morton Homestead in nearby Prospect Park is a fine example of the early Swedish log cabin. Washington was defeated by the British on September 11, 1777, at what is now Brandywine Battlefield State Park.

5 EPHRATA
In 1735 a settlement was built here by members of a semimonastic German religious order, led by the Reverend Johann Conrad Beissel. The gloomy gray buildings of Ephrata Cloisters, restored by the state, include the Sisters' House, the Saal (House of Prayer), the Almonry, and other outbuildings. A summer *Vorspeil* recreates the life and music of early Ephrata. At nearby Lititz, visitors may watch bakers make pretzels in the old-fashioned way. There are many fine old buildings in Lititz.

6 ERIE
This bustling industrial city, Pennsylvania's only Great Lakes port, is built around the site of Fort Presque Isle. The Pennsylvania State Park, comprising the historic Presque Isle peninsula, has seven miles of fine sand beach and affords fine fishing. A monument commemorates Commodore Oliver Hazard Perry's 1813 victory over the English. The Land Lighthouse, originally built in 1813 and replaced in 1858 and 1866, was the first lighthouse on the Great Lakes. The Wayne Blockhouse, a replica of the one in which General "Mad Anthony" Wayne died in 1796, is built over Wayne's original grave and is open to visitors. Displayed near the foot of State Street is the restored U.S.S. *Niagara*, Perry's flagship; nearby is the prow of the U.S.S. *Wolverine*, the nation's first iron-hulled warship, built and launched at Erie in 1843.

7 GETTYSBURG

The Gettysburg National Military Park was the scene of one of the most bloody and decisive battles of the Civil War on July 1–3, 1863. The 25-square-mile park, with its 30 miles of roads through areas where fighting occurred, includes over 1,400 monuments, statues, and markers, and four observation towers, among them a 75-foot-high structure on the edge of the adjoining farm of former President Dwight D. Eisenhower. The cemetery, which President Abraham Lincoln dedicated November 19, 1863, with his famous Gettysburg Address, contains the graves of 4,569 persons. Particularly noteworthy are the Eternal Light Peace Memorial on Oak Hill; General Meade's Headquarters; the Visitor Center; the High Water Mark Monument; the Devil's Den, a Confederate stronghold; and the Meade Statue. The National Park Service has a fine museum there also. Near the park are the National Civil War Wax Museum; the Gettysburg National Museum, with the largest collection of Civil War relics in the world; the Hall of Presidents; and the Lincoln Room Museum at the Wills House on the Square.

8 HARRISBURG

This transportation and manufacturing center has been the state capital since 1812. Its public buildings include the Italian Renaissance State Capitol (1906), with a 272-foot-high gold dome and a marble staircase designed after the Paris Opera; the South Office Building; the Finance Building; and the new William Penn Memorial Museum and Archives Building, which contains Rothermel's *Battle of Gettysburg* mural. About six miles north is the Fort Hunter Museum (built on the site of the original fort), which houses exhibits of Colonial furniture, costumes, and homemaking equipment. About 20 miles west is Carlisle, a strategic point during the Revolutionary and Civil wars. The Carlisle Barracks, established by the British in 1751, is now the home of the U.S. Army War College.

One of the many monuments erected at Gettysburg

KOSTI RUOHOMAA, BLACK STAR

9 HERSHEY

"The Chocolate Capital of the World" was built and planned by Milton S. Hershey in 1903 on what formerly was a cornfield. Its main streets are called Chocolate and Cocoa. Hershey is noted for its recreational, sports, and cultural facilities, such as Hershey Park, which offers boating, swimming, band concerts, and other amusements; the Hershey Museum, with fine exhibits of Colonial and Pennsylvania Dutch items; Hershey Sports Arena and Hershey Stadium, and Hershey Gardens, with over 1,000 varieties of roses. Visitors may tour the Hershey Chocolate Corporation and the Pennsylvania State Police Academy. At Cornwall, about 10 miles east, is the most extensive iron ore deposit in the East, which has been worked since 1735. The Cornwall Charcoal Furnace, which started full operation in 1742, has been restored.

10 JOHNSTOWN

Highwater marks from a flood that claimed more than 2,200 lives and caused an estimated $10 million damage on May 31, 1889, are still visible on some of the older buildings of this steel city. In "the unknown plot of Grandview Cemetery, 777 unidentified flood victims lie under blank headstones. Tourists can ride cable cars of the 895-foot-high Incline Plane to Westmont for a fine view of the city.

11 LANCASTER

This capital of the Pennsylvania Dutch country, the center of one of the nation's most productive agricultural regions, was the capital of the U.S. for one day, September 27, 1777. The picturesque Amish in the area still dress in the style of their ancestors of 300 years ago and drive buggies rather than cars. Tasty Pennsylvania Dutch table delicacies, such as shoo-fly pie and *schmierkäse*, and farm-grown vegetables can be bought at the five Farmers' Markets on Tuesdays, Fridays, and Saturdays. Wheatland (1812), the restored brick Federal home of President James Buchanan, contains many Buchanan family pieces. The nearby Pennsylvania Farm Museum has about 250,000 items, among them, early farm implements, wagons, and spinning wheels. The Amish Farm and House (1805) is furnished and decorated as an old Amish household; the Amish Homestead, three miles east, is a farm still worked by the Amish. From nearby Strasburg visitors can take hour-long, nine-mile rides through the Pennsylvania Dutch countryside on the Strasburg Railroad (chartered in 1832), one of the last regularly scheduled standard-gauge steam passenger trains. At Manheim is the site of the Stiegel glassworks. At the annual Rose Festival in June, a Stiegel descendant receives the yearly "rent" of one red rose for the grounds of the Zion Lutheran Church.

12 NEW HOPE

This charming Delaware River town, founded in 1715, is the center of the Bucks County artists' colony. Tourists can visit the famed Bucks County Playhouse in summer and ride in mule-drawn barges on a reconstructed section of the Old Delaware

Canal, just south of town. An excellent collection of early tools and implements can be viewed at the Mercer Museum in Doylestown. About nine miles south of New Hope is the Washington Crossing State Park, where Washington and 2,400 soldiers crossed the Delaware on Christmas night, 1776. Washington met with his generals in the Thompson-Neely House (1701), and Hessian officers spent their first night of captivity in the Old Ferry Inn (1757). A few miles down the Delaware is Pennsbury Manor (1683), the reconstructed country manor house of William Penn.

13 PHILADELPHIA

Although "the City of Brotherly Love" is one of the nation's great industrial cities and a major port, it retains much of its Colonial charm and is reported to contain more 18th-century buildings than any other English-speaking city in the world except London. Many historic structures associated with the American Revolution have been preserved in the Independence National Historical Park. The Independence Square section includes Independence Hall (1732), home of the Liberty Bell and site of the signing of the Declaration of Independence and framing of the Constitution; Congress Hall (1789); Old City Hall (1791), home of the U.S. Supreme Court until 1800; the American Philosophical Society Building (1789); the first Bank of the U.S. (1795); the Old Custom House (1819–24); and Carpenter's Hall (1770), which housed the First Continental Congress. Other park buildings are Christ Church (1727–54); Old St. Mary's Church (1763), which became one of the nation's first Catholic cathedrals in 1808; Gloria Dei (Old Swede's) Church (1700); St. Joseph's Church (1733); Pennsylvania Hospital (first in America); and the Deshler-Morris House (1792), where Washington lived when Philadelphia was the nation's capital. Other places of interest: Elfreth's Alley and Bladen Court, with quaint, restored 18th-century houses; Betsy Ross House (c. 1700); Powel House (1765); Friends

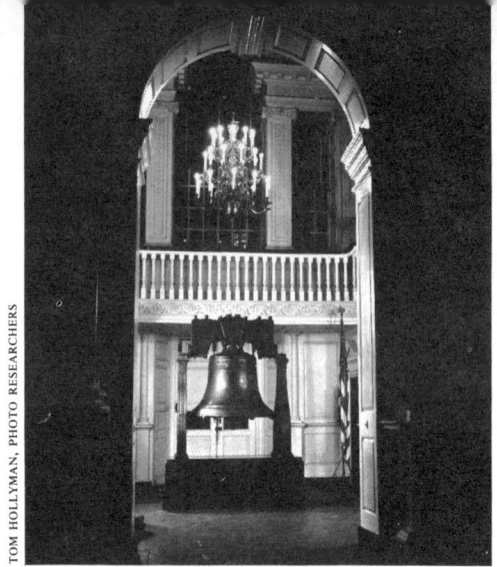

TOM HOLLYMAN, PHOTO RESEARCHERS

The Liberty Bell, in historic Independence Hall

Meeting House (1804); St. George's Methodist Church (1788); the U.S. Mint, where visitors can see coins made; City Hall; Bartram's Mansion and Gardens (1731); Morris Arboretum; Tinicum Marsh Wildlife Preserve; and the Philadelphia Navy Yard. The city's wealth of museums includes the Academy of Natural Sciences; the Pennsylvania Academy of the Fine Arts; the Historical Society of Pennsylvania; the Philadelphia Maritime Museum; the Philadelphia Museum of Art; the University Museum. Several handsome restored 18th-century houses are located in Fairmount Park along the Schuylkill River; Straw Mansion (1798–1830); Woodford (1742–56); Lemon Hill (1770–98); Sweetbriar Mansion (1797); Cedar Grove (1721); Mount Pleasant (1762); Hatfield House (c. 1760–c. 1835); Letitia Street House (1703–15). Noted houses in the Germantown section: Stenton (1728); Grumblethorpe (1754–1808); Hacker House (1772); Wakefield (1798); Cliveden (1761).

14 PITTSBURGH

This great steel city, once called the Smoky City, is known for its spectacular comeback from urban decay and for its smoke control measures. In the Golden Triangle, sparkling glass and steel skyscrapers and a new Point Park have replaced once dismal eyesores. Of particular interest are the new Civic Auditorium; Gateway Center; the Alcoa Building; Gulf Building, the city's highest; Mellon Park; Point State Park; the 42-story Cathedral of Learning at the University of Pittsburgh; and the Stephen Foster Memorial. Carnegie Institute contains fine art galleries and a natural history museum. Nocturnal animals can be found in the Underground Zoo at the Zoological Gardens. The city's only pre-Revolutionary War building is the Blockhouse, built by Colonel Bouquet in 1764. At Ambridge, northwest of the city, are 17 restored buildings of the Old Economy settlement of the Harmony Society, a German communal group.

15 READING

This industrial city is noted for its tasty pretzels. About six miles southeast is the Lincoln Homestead

Colonial houses line Elfreth's Alley, Philadelphia

AMERICAN AIRLINES

(1733), built by Mordecai Lincoln, great-great-grandfather of the President. About nine miles southeast is the Daniel Boone Homestead, a reconstructed stone farmhouse built on the site of the pioneer's log cabin birthplace. The Hopewell Village National Historic Site near Elverson is a fine example of an 18th-century American ironmaking village. Many of the buildings remain as they were when the village produced cannon and ammunition for Washington's men during the Revolution.

16 STROUDSBURG
Capital of the Pocono Mountains vacation country, Stroudsburg and its environs offer year-round sports facilities of all varieties. About three miles east is the Delaware Water Gap, a break in the Kittatinny, or Blue, Mountains. North of the city are scenic Bushkill, Dingmans, and Winona falls. In nearby Milfort is the Pinchot Institute on the Gray Towers Estate, the former home of the late Pennsylvania governor and conservationist, Gifford Pinchot. Many unusual species of animals may be viewed in a natural setting at the Pocono Wild Animal Farm.

17 TITUSVILLE
On August 27, 1859, Edwin L. Drake drilled the nation's first successful oil well on the banks of Oil Creek, so-called because of the oil that sometimes appeared on the surface of the water. In nearby Drake Well Memorial Park is an operating replica of the Drake derrick and engine house. A museum has exhibits dealing with the origin and development of the oil industry.

18 UNIONTOWN
About 11 miles west of this soft coal and coke center is Fort Necessity National Battlefield, where George Washington and a group of Virginians were defeated July 3, 1754, in the first battle of the French and Indian War. The stockade fort was recently rebuilt according to old plans. Relics of the early pioneer period can be seen in the Mt. Washington Tavern (1816). A mile west of the fort at Braddock Park is

The 42-story Cathedral of Learning in Pittsburgh

PHILIP GENDREAU

the grave of General Edward Braddock. Still operating as a tavern is the Century Inn (1794), at Scenery Hill northwest of Uniontown. To the southwest, at New Geneva, is Friendship Hill (1789–1823), the home of Albert Gallatin, Secretary of the Treasury under Jefferson.

19 VALLEY FORGE
Washington's starving soldiers spent the bitter winter of 1777–78 in what is now Valley Forge State Park. In the 2,068-acre memorial to the soldiers' heroism, tourists can see restored soldiers' huts; the Old Camp Schoolhouse (1705), which served as a hospital; Washington's headquarters. The Valley Forge Park Museum and the Valley Forge Museum of American History contain relics of the encampment. The 75-foot-high Observation Tower on Mt. Joy gives a panoramic view of the park. Across the Schuylkill River on Perkiomen Creek is the Audubon Shrine and Wildlife Sanctuary, built around Mill Grove (1762), the first American home of ornithologist John James Audubon.

20 WARREN
Situated at the junction of the Allegheny River and Conewango Creek, this oil center is headquarters for the 471,083-acre Allegheny National Forest, which offers excellent hunting and fishing as well as camping, picnicking, and swimming facilities. About 10 miles east is the Kinzua Dam and Reservoir, scheduled for completion in 1965, which will provide flood control and a huge recreation area. Southeast of Warren, near Kane, the Buffalo Lobo Wolf Park has the only remaining pack of lobo wolves in captivity.

21 WILLIAMSPORT
This birthplace of Little League baseball holds its own world series every August. At Sunbury, to the south, the magazine is all that remains of Fort Augusta, built in 1756 as a French and Indian War outpost. A scale model of the fort can be viewed on the lawn of the Hunter Mansion, which contains many relics of early Sunbury.

22 YORK
This important industrial city was the capital of the American Colonies during the British occupation of Philadelphia in 1777–78; it was here that the Articles of Confederation were adopted. Undergoing restoration are the Plough Tavern (1741), a half-timber structure of medieval German design; and the Gates House (*c.* 1751), where a cabal headed by General Thomas Conway allegedly plotted in 1777 to remove Washington as commander-in-chief of the Continental Army. Quakers still meet regularly at the Friends Meeting House (1766).

> *For further information write to:*
> *Historical and Museum Commission*
> *State Museum Building, Box 232*
> *Harrisburg, Pennsylvania 17108*

INFORMATION ROUNDUP: PENNSYLVANIA

U.S.	Pennsylvania
JAMESTOWN settled **1607**	
	1615 BRULE explores Susquehanna River
	1616 HENDRICKSEN sails up Delaware River
NEW AMSTERDAM settled **1624**	
NEW SWEDEN settled **1638**	
	1643 SWEDES settle Tinicum Island
	1655 DUTCH seize New Sweden
	1664 NEW NETHERLAND captured by British
	1681 PENN granted area
KING WILLIAM'S WAR begins **1689**	
	1701 CHARTER OF LIBERTIES granted by Penn
	1716 IRON FORGE built near Pottstown
FRENCH & INDIAN WAR begins **1754**	
	1755 BRADDOCK defeated on Monongahela R.
TREATY OF PARIS signed **1763**	PONTIAC'S REBELLION
TOWNSHEND ACTS passed **1767**	
	1774 FIRST CONTINENTAL CONGRESS meets
AMERICAN REVOLUTION begins **1775**	SECOND CONTINENTAL CONGRESS meets
	1787 PENNSYLVANIA ratifies U.S. Constitution
	1794 WHISKY REBELLION
	1799 FRIES REBELLION
	1848 MINERS' UNION organized
	1859 OIL WELL drilled near Titusville
CIVIL WAR begins **1861**	
	1863 BATTLE OF GETTYSBURG
	1867 BESSEMER STEEL first produced
	1877 PITTSBURGH RAILROAD STRIKE
	1892 HOMESTEAD STRIKE
	1902 ANTHRACITE STRIKE
CLAYTON ANTITRUST ACT passed **1914**	
STOCK MARKET CRASH **1929**	
WORLD WAR II begins **1941**	
KOREAN WAR begins **1950**	
	1959 STEEL STRIKE

TOPOGRAPHY: Entirely within the Appalachian Mountains, except for narrow strips of plains along Lake Erie in the northwest and the Delaware River in the southeast; west, plateau with deep and narrow valleys, lakes, and woods; west central, the Allegheny Mountains; east central, the Great Appalachian Valley, consisting of hills, rolling uplands, and valleys. Altitudes: high, 3,213 ft.; low, sea level; approx. mean, 1,100 ft.

MAIN RIVERS: Allegheny, Delaware, French Creek, Juniata, Lehigh, Monongahela, Ohio, Schuylkill, Susquehanna, Youghiogheny

LARGEST LAKES: Conemaugh River, Erie, Pymatuning, Tionesta Creek, Wallenpaupack, Youghiogheny River

PRINCIPAL MOUNTAINS: Pocono Mts.; Allegheny Mts.; Jacks Mts.; Blue Mts.; South Mtn.

CLIMATE: Warm summers and cold winters; considerable snowfall in northern and mountainous areas. *Av. temps.*: Philadelphia, July max., 86.5° F; Feb. min., 25.3° F. *Av. ann. precipitation*: Philadelphia, 41.13 in. (snow and sleet, 16.9 in. mean total)

MAJOR CITIES (1960 census): Philadelphia (2,002,512); Pittsburgh (604,332); Erie (138,440); Scranton (111,443); Allentown (108,347)

NATIONAL FOREST: Allegheny

NATIONAL PARKS: Fort Necessity National Battlefield; Gettysburg National Cemetery; Gettysburg National Military Park; Independence National Historical Park

NATIONAL HISTORIC SITES: Gloria Dei Church, Hopewell Village

STATE PARKS: 64 parks; 2 state forest monuments; 7 natural areas; 8 historical parks; 22 historic properties

UNIVERSITIES: Bucknell; Carnegie Institute of Technology; Dropsie College for Hebrew and Cognate Learning; Duquesne; Hahnemann Medical College; Jefferson Medical College of Philadelphia; Lehigh; Pennsylvania; Pennsylvania State; Pittsburgh; Temple; Villanova; Woman's Medical College of Pennsylvania

NICKNAME: Keystone State
MOTTO: Virtue, Liberty, and Independence
ORIGIN OF NAME: "Penn's Woods," for Sir William Penn
AREA (1960): 45,333 sq. mi. (water, 326 sq. mi.); *rank*, 33
POPULATION (1960 census): 11,319,366; *rank*, 3
CAPITAL: Harrisburg
DATE U.S. CONSTITUTION RATIFIED: Dec. 12, 1787; *rank*, 2
FINANCE (Fiscal 1962): Revenue, $2,412,032,000
Expenditure, $2,231,038,000
U.S. REPRESENTATIVES: 27
STATE FLOWER: Mountain Laurel
STATE TREE: Hemlock
STATE BIRD: Ruffed Grouse

THUMBNAIL HISTORY

The two major arteries into Pennsylvania from the sea—the Delaware and Susquehanna rivers—were probably first explored within the area of the present state by Etienne Brulé, who journeyed down the Susquehanna to its mouth in 1615–16, and Cornelius Hendricksen, who sailed up the Delaware to or beyond the mouth of the Schuylkill River in 1616. A Swedish settlement on Tinicum Island in the Delaware was founded in 1643 and served as the capital of New Sweden until the Dutch seized the colony in 1655. The British, in turn, ousted the Dutch nine years later, and in 1681 Charles II granted almost all of Pennsylvania to the Quaker William Penn, whose guarantee of religious freedom drew many immigrants. Settlement of western Pennsylvania did not proceed as rapidly until Indian hostilities and rivalry with the French over the Ohio Valley fur trade ended with the French and Indian War of 1754–63 and the Treaty of Stanwix with the Iroquois in 1768. Pennsylvania was a leader in opposition to British Colonial policies, and the First and Second Continental Congresses were held in 1774 and 1775 at Philadelphia, which was the capital of the new United States from 1790 to 1800. Discontent over Federal taxation brought about the Whisky Rebellion of 1794 and the Fries ("Hot Water") Rebellion of 1799. A center of the abolitionist movement, Pennsylvania was a strong supporter of the Union in the Civil War, and a major battle was fought at Gettysburg in July, 1863. After the war, the expansion of coal mining and the steel industry was accompanied by mounting labor protest, which resulted in the Pittsburgh railroad strike of 1877, the Homestead steel strike of 1892, and the anthracite coal field strikes of 1897 and 1902. Unemployment was very high during the 1930's, but Pennsylvania industries worked to capacity in World War II and the Korean War. In recent years there has been considerable unemployment in the coal fields.

GOVERNMENT and POLITICS

The governor and state senators are elected for four-year terms; state representatives serve for two years. Vote in Presidential elections 1900–1964: Rep., 11; Dem., 5; Progressive, 1.

ECONOMY

With coal, iron ore, and lime at hand, Pennsylvania early developed into an important producer of iron and steel, and although now it must obtain most of the ore from the Lake Superior deposits, the state (particularly Pittsburgh) is the leading manufacturer of primary metals in the U.S. It is also among the top-ranking states in almost every other major industrial category, such as machinery, fabricated metal goods, food products, textiles, apparel, and chemicals. Virtually all the country's output of anthracite coal comes from Pennsylvania, and it is one of the chief sources of bituminous coal, cement, and lime. Agriculture, especially dairy and poultry farming, is prosperous. The chief crops are hay, corn, wheat, and oats. Philadelphia is a major commercial center, and the Port of Philadelphia is an important artery for foreign trade.

TRANSPORTATION AND COMMUNICATION (1962)
RAILROADS: 8,880 line miles
ROADS: 109,908 miles (22,541 miles nonsurfaced)
MOTOR VEHICLES REGISTERED: 4,486,802
AIRPORTS (as of Jan. 1): 427 (138 general)
RADIO STATIONS: 157 AM, 67 FM
TELEVISION STATIONS: 19
DAILY NEWSPAPERS (1963): 119

TIMBER (1958)
STUMPAGE CUT: 118,250,000 cu. ft.
VALUE OF STUMPAGE CUT: $10,000,000

FURS (1961–62)
PRINCIPAL ANIMAL CATCH: Muskrat (377,571); raccoon (51,062); opossum (9,813); mink (7,999); fox (4,471); beaver (4,136)

PENNSYLVANIA AND U.S. PERSONAL INCOME (1962)
By major sources as per cent of total
U.S. TOTAL: $439,661,000,000
PENNSYLVANIA TOTAL: $26,887,000,000

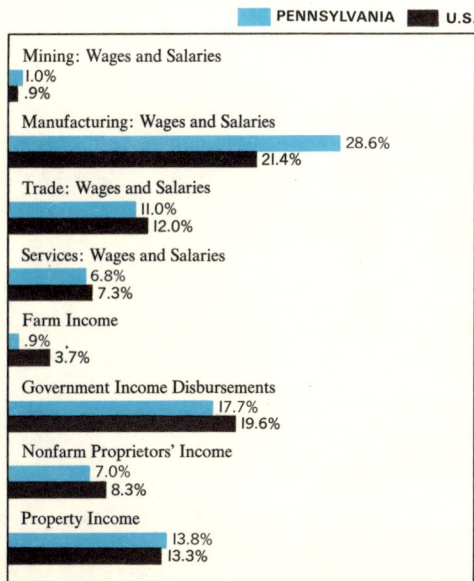

■ PENNSYLVANIA ■ U.S.

Mining: Wages and Salaries
1.0%
.9%

Manufacturing: Wages and Salaries
28.6%
21.4%

Trade: Wages and Salaries
11.0%
12.0%

Services: Wages and Salaries
6.8%
7.3%

Farm Income
.9%
3.7%

Government Income Disbursements
17.7%
19.6%

Nonfarm Proprietors' Income
7.0%
8.3%

Property Income
13.8%
13.3%

PRINCIPAL MANUFACTURES (1962 est.)

Industry	Employees	Value Added* ($1,000)
Primary metal industries	216,672	2,426,364
Food and kindred products	108,002	1,237,723
Machinery, except electrical	115,009	1,211,133
Electrical machinery	108,505	1,152,952
Fabricated metal products	106,515	1,029,492
Chemicals and allied products	46,583	947,347
Apparel and related products	173,459	825,027
Printing and publishing	65,805	632,934
Stone, clay, and glass products	59,809	623,421
Transportation equipment	61,584	596,804
Paper and allied products	38,841	451,601

*Value added by manufacture, adjusted

PRINCIPAL MINERALS EXTRACTED (1962 est.)

Product	Quantity (1,000 short tons)	Value ($1,000)
Coal (bituminous)	65,315	331,298
Coal (anthracite)	16,894	134,094
Portland cement (1,000 barrels)	38,463	127,969
Stone	48,144	82,087
Natural gas (1,000,000 cu. ft.)	90,053	24,494
Petroleum (1,000 barrels)	5,225	23,878
Sand and gravel	14,419	23,587
Lime	1,104	16,647
Clays	2,893	12,815
Items that cannot be disclosed	—	32,966

AGRICULTURE (1963 est.)

Product	Harvested Acres	Quantity (1,000)	Value ($1,000)
Hay	2,113,000	3,217 tons	117,420
Corn for grain	812,000	43,036 bu.	61,111
Wheat	487,000	14,854 bu.	25,252
Oats	589,000	32,395 bu.	24,296
Potatoes	38,000	7,376 cwt.	16,355
Apples	—	8,000 bu.	13,920
Cattle & calves (1962)	—	408,310 lbs.	79,740
Hogs (1962)	—	160,653 lbs.	27,793
Dairy products (1962)	—	—	323,956*
Poultry & eggs (1962)	—	—	145,800*

*Gross farm income

TOTAL VALUE ADDED BY MANUFACTURE, ADJUSTED (1962 est.): $13,123,364,000
TOTAL VALUE OF MINERALS EXTRACTED (1962 est.): $823,152,000
TOTAL CASH RECEIPTS FROM FARMING (1962 est.): $809,487,000

RHODE ISLAND

When the navigator Giovanni da Verrazano discovered Block Island in 1524, he named it for the Greek Isle of Rhodes in the Mediterranean Sea, and in time the name was applied to Aquidneck Island and thence, finally, to the entire state. The recollection of Rhodes turned out to be surprisingly apt, because the early history of Rhode Island, like that of ancient Greece, was formed by a relentless drive for spiritual self-realization and by the omnipresence of the sea (opposite). In the Colonial period Rhode Island was a haven for religious dissenters and minorities, and despite its small size it became one of the most vigorous and successful seafaring provinces in America. Then, in the 19th century, the textile industry was established, bringing with it the drabness of factories, economic instability, and a period of travail. But old traditions have persevered, and the Union's smallest state is today reconstructing itself in the spirit of its great past.

WOONSOCKET

Pascoag Reservoir

CENTRAL FALLS
PAWTUCKET

EAST PROVIDENCE

PROVIDENCE
CRANSTON

Scituate Reservoir

WARREN

BRISTOL

WARWICK

Flat River Reservoir

Prudence Island

Stafford Pond

PORTSMOUTH

Conanicut Island

Rhode Island

HOPE VALLEY

NEWPORT

Pawcatuck River

Worden Pond

NARRAGANSETT

RHODE ISLAND SOUND

WESTERLY

Watchaug Pond

Point Judith

BLOCK ISLAND SOUND

ATLANTIC OCEAN

Block Island

0   10   20
SCALE OF MILES

A TRADITION OF TOLERANCE

Roger Williams fled from Salem in midwinter.

O n top of the State Capitol in Providence is a statue representing the Independent Man, who is depicted resolutely holding a spear in one hand, while the other rests firmly on an anchor. And inside the giant dome is inscribed a quotation from the Roman historian Tacitus: "Rara temporum felicitas ubi sentire quae velis et quae sentias dicere licet." (Rare are the felicitous times when one is permitted to think as one likes and say what one thinks.)

The 17th century was hardly such a felicitous epoch, and the founding of Rhode Island is a testimony to the audacious will and heroic courage displayed by men and women who dared maintain an independent spirit in any matter of conscience, particularly religion. Foremost among those intrepid souls was Roger Williams. He had left England in 1630 at the age of 27 rather than put up with the theological strictures imposed by the Anglican Church, and then within a short time after his arrival in Massachusetts got into a political fight with the intolerant theocrats of Salem, who had him banished from the Bay Colony by the Massachusetts General Court. Rather than return to England he fled into the wilderness in mid-January, 1636, and after six months of wandering, during which he was joined by four other men and a boy, bought some land from the Indians on the Moshassuck River, where he founded Providence.

Two years later John Clarke and William Coddington, followers of the redoubtable mystic Anne Hutchinson, planted another settlement at Portsmouth. Shortly afterward, they were joined by Mrs. Hutchinson herself, who had been denounced as a spiritual "leper" and banished by the Massachusetts General Court for her views on the intuitive revelation of God's love. Political squabbles between her and Coddington led to the latter's withdrawal from the group and his founding of Newport in 1639. A fourth community, Warwick, was established in 1643 by Samuel Gorton, whose rancorous disposition not only brought his banishment from Massachusetts but even made him unwelcome in Providence.

Rhode Island—or the Colony of Rhode Island and Providence Plantations, as the communities were known after they united under a charter granted in 1644—naturally attracted a wide variety of religious dissenters. The first congregation of Baptists in America was founded in 1639 by a group of fervid dissenters from the Anglican Church, and the sect gradually began to prosper in Rhode Island's tolerant atmosphere. In 1764 Rhode Island

College, later renamed Brown University, was founded by the Baptists, and in 1775 they built in Providence their renowned First Meeting House, a gracious, simple structure with a magnificent spire constructed after a design by James Gibbs.

Quakers also came to the Colony, and even though Roger Williams furiously attacked their principles, they were permitted to stay. In the 1650's, about the time of the arrival of the Quakers, a group of Sephardic (Spanish-Portuguese) Jews settled in Newport. The Touro Synagogue, built in 1763, is the second oldest Jewish house of worship in the United States and is still used for services by the Jeshuet Israel Congregation. In 1946 the building was designated a national historic site.

Roman Catholics, however, were not given so generous a reception, despite the provision in a new charter granted by Charles II in 1663 that "all and every person and persons may from tyme to tyme and at all tymes hereafter freelye and fullye enjoye his and their own judgements in matters of religious concernments." From 1664 to 1783 Roman Catholics were deprived of the right to vote, and militant Protestants made every attempt to keep the "papists" from opening parishes. Ironically, of the 661,263 Rhode Islanders counted as regularly attending church in 1963, 525,274 were Roman Catholic because of the immigration of French Canadians, Irish, Slavs, and Italians in the 19th century. The Episcopalians, descendants of the Anglicans from whom many of the early settlers had fled, had 51,197 churchgoers, while the old dissenting sects, the Baptists and Congregationalists, had only 23,668 and 13,382.

The statue of the Independent Man stands watch over Providence from the top of the Capitol.

THE DILIGENT RHODE ISLANDERS

ERIC M. SANFORD

The machinery used in the Slater Mill (above) was primitive compared to the modern electronics (below) and textile (center) equipment, but silverworking (far right) is unchanged.

One attribute common to most of the stern Protestant sects was an abhorrence of idleness. To "make the earth fructify" they believed to be as inviolable an obligation for all godly men as attention to many other scriptural commandments. With characteristic diligence the Rhode Islanders early developed a thriving economy based largely on agriculture and commerce, but after Samuel Slater built a water-driven cotton spinner at Pawtucket in 1790, mills sprang up along the rivers flowing into Narragansett Bay, and Rhode Island quickly became a leader in the manufacture of textiles. Shipbuilding had been important since the 17th century, and by 1880 the state's jewelry-making industry, centered in Providence, was the foremost in the country. Agricul-

LEFT AND RIGHT: *Providence Journal–Bulletin*

ture continued to prosper, but, of course, became less important relatively, until in 1962 farming accounted for only about 1 per cent of all employment in the state and .3 per cent of personal income.

Textile manufacturing is still Rhode Island's leading industry. It has been in a serious decline for about four decades, however, due primarily to competition from the rapidly expanding textile industries of North and South Carolina and other Southern states, where labor costs are lower and the newer factories have more automated equipment. Since 1950 employment in the various aspects of textile production has decreased by more than 50 per cent, and between 1958 and 1962 alone the number of firms in the industry dropped from 417 to 394. Other traditional industries, such as the manufacture of jewelry and silverware and rubber products, have suffered setbacks, but the consequences have not been so critical.

To some extent the depressing effects of the decline in textiles have been offset by the growth of new industries. At the end of 1962, for example, there were 24 electronics firms and 260 concerns making nonelectrical machinery, as compared to 12 and 255, respectively, in 1958. Financial backing for plant construction given by the Rhode Island Industrial Building Authority, which was established in 1958, has been an important factor in this expansion. But the economy of the smallest state is precarious, and unemployment—6.4 per cent in 1964—is still higher than the national average.

THE GORHAM COMPANY

Large commercial structures are interspersed with the historic buildings in downtown Providence.

DECLINE AND RENEWAL

On the afternoon of March 2, 1775, the clarion voice of the town crier sounded through the narrow streets of Providence, calling upon "all true friends of their country, lovers of freedom, and haters of shackles" to gather at Market Square, where the local patriots had built a high bonfire out of 300 pounds of tea in protest against the tax favors given the British-owned East India Company. Unlike the Boston Tea Party 14 months before, this gesture of defiance was somewhat gratuitous, since Rhode Island was already in virtual rebellion against the mother country. At Newport in 1769 a British revenue sloop, the *Liberty*, which lucklessly had run aground on a shoal, was sunk, and three years after that the *Gaspee*, also a revenue ship, was put to the torch in Narragansett Bay.

The tiny colony's ardent patriotism was in part an outgrowth of the fiery religious libertarianism of the early settlers, but it also stemmed in a large measure from commercial considerations. After the construction of the first Providence wharf in 1680, the city rapidly developed into a busy port specializing in the famous triangular trade, which in this instance consisted of bartering New England-made rum in Africa for slaves, who were sold to the West Indian planters, from whom, in turn, molasses was bought for the New England rum distilleries. British mercantilist restrictions on trade with foreigners were especially detestable to the merchants of Providence because of their profitable business with the French West Indies, and when the Revolution broke out a month after the Providence Tea Party, the people of the city were unsurpassed in their support of the American cause.

But in the 19th century Rhode Island underwent a great change. The restive independence of spirit that had characterized the first century and a half of its history for a long while, gave way to conservatism and exclusiveness. Suffrage was limited to the wealthier landholders until an armed rebellion led by Thomas Wilson Dorr in 1842 finally brought about the adoption of a modern constitution to replace as the state's fundamental law the antiquated charter granted by Charles II to the Rhode Island Colony in 1663. As industry expanded, immigration, first from French Canada and Ireland and then from Continental Europe, swelled the population. The newcomers, most of them Catholic, were disdained by the Protestants, and because of the lower wages paid the immigrants, considerable resentment developed among the American workers. Political control of the state now passed to a handful of industrialists, and this, coupled with friction between the various ethnic groups, retarded the organization of labor unions and the passage of social legislation. Gradually, though, the old *élan* began to return, and Rhode Island is now undertaking the task of rejuvenation.

Providence typifies some of the problems confronting the state. The city is badly overcrowded (Rhode Island is the most densely populated state in the country), and drab commercial buildings, factories, and railroad yards were erected without regard for the architectural beauty of the city's many important historic sites. Moreover, the protracted depression in the textile industry has had a particularly severe effect in the capital.

In the past few years, though, Providence businessmen and city officials have taken decisive action to stop the deterioration. As part of a broad urban renewal program, plans are being made to relocate the New Haven Railroad terminal and tracks, and an industrial park has been established on the outskirts of the city. Under the auspices of the Providence Preservation Society, historic Benefit Street is being restored, and money has been raised through public subscription to save the Colonial mansions of the East Side. Brown University, a center of Providence cultural life, has constructed a new physics and engineering building and an auditorium, as well as other facilities. The rapidly proceeding renovation of Providence has set an example for the whole state, and similar programs have been started in a number of other Rhode Island cities.

Brown graduates march to the Baptist Church.

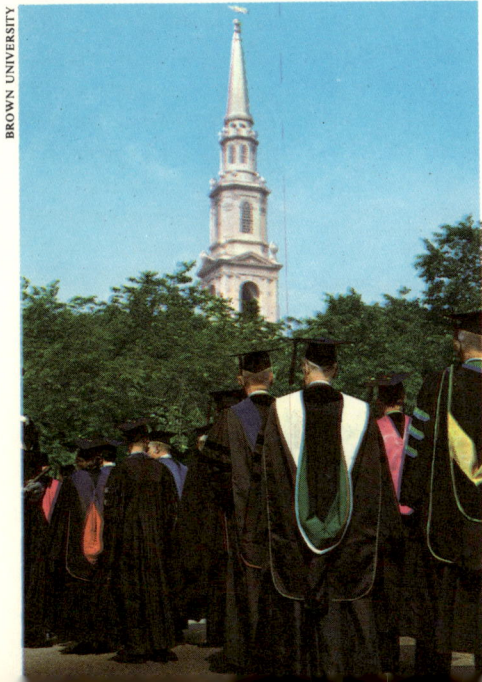

Benefit Street dates from the Colonial era.

QUEENLY NEWPORT

Newport has always been an anomaly among the cities of Rhode Island. Situated on Rhode (Aquidneck) Island in Narragansett Bay, it is not only physically separated from the rest of the state, but in its development, especially since the Revolution, has followed its own inimitable course.

Shipbuilding began there as early as 1646, barely seven years after the founding of the city, and within a short time local shipowners were reaping enormous profits from the ignominious traffic in slaves. Newport itself became an important slave center, and for this reason, in addition to its gentle summer climate and propitious location on the sea, aristocratic Southerners and West Indian planters began, about the middle of the 18th century, to take vacations in the congenial city.

When after the Revolution the slave trade became illegal and most of Newport's other commerce shifted to New York, the city went into a decline. A few attempts were made to establish textile mills, but the industry never took root, as it did in Providence and elsewhere. About the 1830's, however, Newport's

The Newport beaches have long been popular.

TONY RAY-JONES

popularity as a resort for Southerners began to revive, and by the 1850's a veritable boom was under way. After the Civil War, wealthy Northerners replaced the now impoverished Southern gentry as the principal tourists. Then about 1890 Newport entered the Gilded Age.

For about six or seven weeks every summer, Newport became the scene of the most lavish and extravagant social life the country had ever seen. In the so-called cottages—actually fabulous mansions—built by John Jacob Astor, Harry Lehr, William K. Vanderbilt, and other multimillionaires on the cliffs overlooking the sea, a series of balls costing as much as $200,000 each, dinner parties, and other prodigious diversions were held by and for the elite of the Social Register. One society matron, Mrs. Pembroke Jones, allotted $300,000 a season for entertaining, and Harry Lehr, the buffoon of the set, once gave an elaborate dinner party for about a hundred dogs, who were served such canine delicacies as fricassee of bones and stewed liver and rice. World War I and the adoption of the income tax amendment to the Constitution in 1913 brought these wasteful extravaganzas to an end. A "Newport Season" still exists and the *haute monde* still gives balls (though these are mostly benefits for charity), but some of the palatial "cottages" have been torn down, and others, like the Elms—which was barely saved from destruction by the Newport Preservation Society—and the Breakers, are now open to the public for inspection.

One particularly salutary effect of Newport's unusual history is that since the Revolution the old section of the town has suffered comparatively little change and remains much as it was in Colonial times. About 400 examples of 17th- and 18th-century architecture survive.

Millionaires built their palatial "cottages" along the cliffs overlooking the sea at Newport (above). The Breakers, Cornelius Vanderbilt's 70-room mansion (below), is now open to the public.

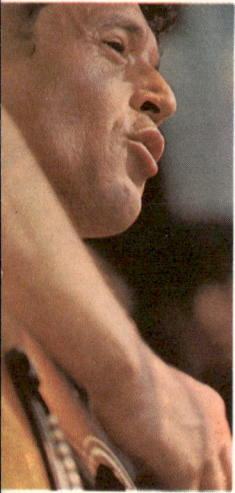

NEWPORT JAZZ

With their city barely restored to calm after the shenanigans of the Gilded Age, the sedate residents of Newport in 1954 warily undertook to be host every July 4th to a jazz festival. From all over the country came bespectacled connoisseurs, teenagers in bluejeans, and other jazzophiles to hear such masters as Louis Armstrong and Duke Ellington. But as the festival's renown spread, the city's hotels and restaurants were increasingly hard put to accommodate the crowds. For three or four days the streets and beaches would be packed with boisterous fans, who sometimes could not even get tickets to the jam sessions. Finally, one hot night during the 1960 festival a riot broke out. When it was over, Newport streets were littered with beer cans and broken glass. Although there have been no recurrences of violence in the years since, the town fathers in late 1964 decided to deny the jazz festival further use of Freebody Park, a sports field where the concerts had been held. A folk festival, which was held in 1959 and 1960 but then lapsed until its revival in 1963, has also been deprived of its home at the park. The festivals in early 1965 were still seeking a site in Rhode Island—but this time as far away as possible from the towns.

RHODE ISLAND
FLORA AND FAUNA

BIRDS

1) Rhode Island Red; 2) Barn Swallow;
3) Least Flycatcher;
4) Short-billed Marsh Wren;
5) Black Guillemot;* 6) Black Scoter*

ANIMAL LIFE

1) White-footed Mouse;
2) Long-tailed Weasel; 3) Muskrat;
4) Northern Starfish;
5) Horseshoe Crab; 6) Blue Crab

FLOWERS

1) Violet; 2) Periwinkle;
3) Seaside Goldenrod; 4) Meadow Beauty;
5) Green-headed Coneflower

TREES

1) Maple; 2) Cockspur Thorn;
3) Cherry Birch; 4) Hickory;
5) Glaucous Willow

*Migratory

GUY COHELEACH

1040

SMOKE STACKS AND GENERAL STORES

A group of Rhode Island's surviving Indians don costumes for native ceremonies at Charlestown.

Of the four original settlements of Rhode Island, only two—Providence and Warwick—continued to play significant roles in the state's economic development after the Revolution. Warwick, like Providence, became one of the principal industrial centers, and although the area along the Pawtuxet River where most of the city's textile mills are located was incorporated as the separate town of West Warwick in 1913, Warwick itself in 1962 still had 100 manufacturing firms, most of them producers of electronics equipment, textiles, and various other light goods. However, the city, which is actually an agglomeration of villages and residential neighborhoods, has now assumed the character of a suburb of Providence.

The fate of Rhode Island's cities was, of course, determined primarily by whether or not the textile industry took root in them. Pawtucket, where Samuel Slater constructed his power spinning frame and in 1793 established the first successful mill for spinning cotton thread in America, was a natural site for building mills because of the abundant water power afforded by the Blackstone River. On the basis of a thriving Colonial metal-working industry, which had also developed because of the ready water power, machine and tool manufacturing (primarily for the needs of the mills) became important and enabled the city to weather the violent fluctuations to which the textile industry is exceedingly susceptible. Similarly, Woonsocket, on the upper Blackstone River, and Cranston, on the Pawtuxet, became not only textile centers but also producers of machinery and tools. The former city, though, was particularly hard hit by the flight of textile firms after World War II to the South, where labor costs are lower. To arrest the consequent general economic decline, a group of businessmen have organized the Industrial Development Foundation of Greater Woonsocket to find tenants for vacated mills and raise capital funds for a 60-acre industrial park, which has now been opened at North Smithfield, just outside of Woonsocket.

Other communities that in Colonial days were the largest and most dynamic in Rhode Island were pinched off in their growth because the textile industry either never became established or for one reason or another failed to expand. Portsmouth, one of the four original settlements, is now merely a small township of some 8,000 inhabitants. Shipbuilding flourished there in the Colonial period, but in the 19th century the most important activity, except for some coal mining, was fishing. Bristol, a town of about 15,000 people, was the fourth-ranking seaport in the United States as late as 1812, and then, after its commerce was ruined by the War of 1812, the energetic merchants made over their ships into whalers. Shipbuilding continued to be important until the second half of the 19th

A quiet, tree-shaded street in Wickford village

century, and some textile mills located there, but even though both industries have persevered, they are now very modest. There are now seven textile mills, and racing yachts are built at the famous Herreshoff boat yard. A few villages—like Wickford, with its snug harbor and yacht basin, and Little Compton, near which in the 1850's was bred the Rhode Island Red Hen (a staple of the American poultry industry)—have simply gone on more or less as they were before the Revolution, timeless, peaceful, retaining much of their Colonial character. As in many New England towns, life centers around the general store and the church. But some places that owe their existence entirely to textile mills founded in the 19th century all but expired when the mills closed down. In the Blackstone River valley, extending from Central Falls to Woonsocket, is a string of stark, unattractive villages, ghostly testimonials to the singular influence that the textile industry had upon the history of Rhode Island.

General stores are still seen in many villages.

RHODE ISLAND LEGENDS AND LORE

A corn bread so delicious that it would make children smile 24 hours a day and have them laughing in their sleep? That's what Shepherd Tom Hazard, the Rhode Island essayist, claimed for the huckleberry johnnycakes made from native corn ground between millstones of Narragansett granite. He reported that "the faces of little boys and girls that were fed during the whole berry season on half and half huckleberry jonny-cake grew into the shape of a smile that remained until the berries came again the next summer."

If Rhode Island's Revolutionary War hero, General Nathanael Greene, had been fed on the johnnycake of the Rhode Island coastal counties instead of on the inferior corn cakes of inland Kent County, Tom claimed, "he would never have let George Washington get ahead of him." And as to an out-of-state product like Boston's famous brown bread—well. He had brought home a loaf, Tom recalled, but after the first mouthful his family refused to eat it. So the loaf was placed in the pig's trough as the old sow was accustomed to a scrap or two of rye and

Indian as a treat. "The old creature—which had not been fed that morning—dove her nose greedily into it; but at the first taste she dropped the morsel, and regarding me askance, with a suspicious and sinister expression in her eye, she hastened to a stagnant, muddy pool in the corner of the yard and rinsed her mouth."

The small size of Rhode Island only seems to inspire a greater loyalty and pride among its citizens. Given the limited resources of the state, Yankee ingenuity could be counted on to turn every asset to an advantage. No matter how small a stream flowed through a farmer's land, he could often figure a way to put a cotton mill beside it and have its water run his machinery. History records one factory built on a tiny branch of the Pawtuxet River. The brook had little water but a good swift running current. "One day when the machinery was running full speed," a 19th-century historian wrote, "all at once the wheel almost stopped. The help ran out to see what the matter was. *They found a cow drinking the water that ought to run on to the wheel.*"

No Rhode Islanders were more ingen-

JOHN ALCORN

ious than the inhabitants of Block Island, nine miles offshore in the Atlantic. In order to scrape up a living on the island, where there was not enough arable land to go around, its citizens used to farm the shoreline for salvage from wrecked ships. The islanders stationed themselves on the beach with poles that had bent nails at the end to hook out of the water any floating goods that appeared valuable. Everyone on the island—from old men to little children—had a "wreck hook," and to prevent fights the islanders agreed on a standard length for the poles.

One day a preacher from the mainland showed up on the island. Block Island was willing to hear his sermons but not to pay for them, and the poor man was soon starving to death. Dismayed at the prospect of having to pay for his funeral expenses, the islanders held a town meeting. There was no question of giving any money to him. Someone thought perhaps after a big catch the town could spare him a fish. Others suggested that half a dozen onions and maybe a potato or two would keep him alive for a month. Finally, a decision was reached. The preacher would

be allowed a wreck hook one and a half inches longer than anyone else's.

One of the strangest tales told about Block Island is of a ghost ship called the *Palatine*, which dozens of islanders have sworn they have seen. By one account, the captain of the *Palatine*, a ship loaded with German emigrants in the 18th century, was murdered by a mutinous crew while at sea, and the passengers were forced to pay exorbitant sums for food and drink. Many died of starvation and the rest were robbed of their valuables before the crew deserted the ship. The *Palatine* drifted onto the reefs of Block Island and was wrecked. A dozen of the surviving passengers were rescued by the islanders, but one half-crazed woman was forgotten. As the wreckers towed the ship away, a hurricane began to blow and the *Palatine* was cut away from the towlines and set on fire. As it floated out to sea, the wreckers heard the cries of the insane woman, shrieking among the flames. In years after, when a blazing ship appeared off the coast, old men would shake their heads, knowing that a storm would soon be rocking Block Island.

1045

On a breezy day in summer the waters off the Rhode Island coast are inevitably dotted with sailboats and pleasure craft of every description (top), except when an area has been cleared for some exclusive race or regatta, such as the Bermuda or America's Cup international yachting contests. Spearfishing and skindiving (above) are also very popular summertime sports. But for the men attending the Naval War College or the various other training schools at the Newport Naval Base, seafaring is a hard and serious business (right).

1046

THE SEA ALL AROUND

In one respect, at least, Rhode Island has been constant throughout its history. Despite the overwhelming importance of industry, the economy of the state and the daily life of the population continue to be enormously influenced by the sea. Every major city, except Woonsocket, is either on the ocean or on the salty waters of Narragansett Bay and its inlets, and more than 25 per cent of the total land area is tidewater. On a few occasions disastrous floods caused by hurricanes have inundated large sections of the state. (The worst in recent times occurred on September 21, 1938, when a tidal wave flooded downtown Providence with 13.9 feet of water, but hurricanes in 1944, 1954, 1955, and 1960 also caused considerable damage.) Providence is still a major port, especially for the receipt of petroleum. Boatmaking, fishing, seaside resorts, and—above all—U.S. Navy installations in the state directly and indirectly provide employment for a large number of Rhode Islanders.

On Rhode Island are the headquarters of the sprawling Newport Naval Base, which actually includes 14 distinct commands plus seven associate commands, with installations scattered throughout the bay area. On the west side of the bay is the Quonset Point Naval Air Station, home port of the aircraft carriers U.S.S. *Lake Champlain* and *Essex*, and nearby at Davisville is the U.S. Naval Construction Battalion Center, headquarters of the Seabees. The U.S. Atlantic Fleet Cruiser-Destroyer Force also docks at Rhode Island, and a new nuclear submarine base is scheduled to open at Melville in 1966. Altogether, 38,909 military and civilian personnel were employed at the Newport Naval Base in 1963, approximately 10,000 more people than worked in the state's textile manufacturing concerns. The Over-haul and Repair Department of the Quonset Point Naval Air Station is Rhode Island's largest single employer.

Shipbuilding, of course, in no way compares with the thriving industry of the Colonial period, but the seafaring traditions of Rhode Island have made it a gathering place for yachtsmen and sailing enthusiasts from all over the country and the construction of pleasure craft and the repair and servicing of boats are busy seasonal activities. During the summer of 1964 dozens of races, regattas, and cruises were scheduled, among them the famous America's Cup international yacht race, which has been held at Newport since 1930 whenever a challenge to the United States by the yachtsmen of some other country is accepted by the omnipotent New York Yacht Club. Of the 20 firms making boats in 1964—three more than a decade earlier—all but one specialized in pleasure craft.

In fact, Rhode Island's excellent summer recreational facilities constitute one of the state's major sources of badly needed out-of-state money. The cool breezes of Block Island, about nine miles off the coast, make it one of the most popular resorts in the East, and Watch Hill, Narragansett Pier, and Jamestown have long been summertime favorites. Although commercial fishing, like shipbuilding, has declined in relative importance, the waters off Rhode Island are considered by fishermen to be among the best sporting grounds along the Atlantic coast. Every year, usually in September, an average of 140 competing boats assemble at the tiny village of Galilee near Narragansett for the Atlantic Tuna Tournament. Further expansion of the tourist industry through development of recreational facilities is an important part of Rhode Island's program for economic recovery.

RHODE ISLAND PLACES OF INTEREST

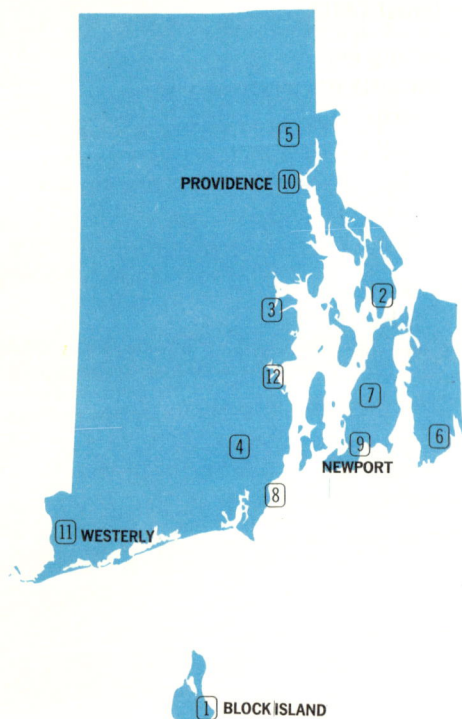

BLOCK ISLAND

1 BLOCK ISLAND

A resort island, located about nine miles off the coast of Rhode Island. Near Southeast Light rise the spectacular Mohegan Bluffs. Deep-sea fishing and bird watching are popular, as is swimming at Block Island State Beach. Ferries cross over from Point Judith, Providence, Newport, and New London, Connecticut.

2 BRISTOL

Many of the America's Cup winners have been built in Bristol's Herreshoff boat yard. Situated on a peninsula between Mount Hope and Narragansett bays, this historic seafaring town has a large number of fine old homes, particularly along Hope Street. The Bristol Art Gallery is one of the Northeast's finest small-town galleries. The Indian leader King Philip had his headquarters at Mount Hope; and there is an interesting collection of Indian artifacts and relics housed in the Haffenreffer Museum. Colt Drive offers a scenic route along the shore; there is swimming at adjoining Bristol Town Beach. Ferries for Prudence Island, where the late President John F. Kennedy and others received PT-boat training, dock at Church Street.

3 EAST GREENWICH

This old residential town, on the western shore of Narragansett Bay, has some handsome Colonial houses. Most historic is the General James Mitchell Varnum House (1773), with period furnishings. Also of interest: the Varnum Memorial Armory, containing a military and naval museum; the Armory of the Kentish Guards, chartered in 1774; Kent County Courthouse (1750). There are recreational facilities in Warwick's Goddard Memorial State Park, east of town. To the northwest, in Coventry, stands the General Nathanael Greene Homestead (1770), home of the Revolutionary War hero.

4 KINGSTON

A quiet, historic village and the seat of the University of Rhode Island. Buildings of interest include the Helme House (1802) and Kingston Inn (c. 1757), now used by the university. The Museum of Primitive Culture, in Peace Dale, is worth visiting. And less than 10 miles away, the Great Swamp Fight Monument commemorates one of the most savage battles of King Philip's War (1675–76). Well-marked paths wind through the Great Swamp Wildlife Reservation; to the south are some of the state's finest ocean beaches.

5 LINCOLN

Named after Abraham Lincoln, this township just north of Providence has a fine example of a "stone-ender," the Eleazer Arnold House (c. 1687). The house stands near the entrance to Lincoln Woods State Park, a heavily wooded 627-acre recreation area. In the environs: Lincoln Downs race track; a 1703 Friends Meeting House; Limerock, a picturesque limestone quarrying community.

6 LITTLE COMPTON

An attractive, spacious summer resort community with numerous historic landmarks, old farms, and summer residences. Elizabeth Alden Pabodie, daughter of Priscilla and John Alden, is buried in the old churchyard near the tree-sheltered common. The Amasa Gray House is a picturesque 17th-century "block house," with wings added later. Three miles away, in Adamsville, stands a monument to the famous Rhode Island Red Hen; to the south lies Sakonnet, a quaint fishing village.

7 MIDDLETOWN

Whitehall, a farmhouse possibly dating to the late 17th century, was acquired in 1729 and enlarged by the noted Irish philosopher George Berkeley, Dean of Derry; it has been handsomely restored. Purgatory, a remarkable chasm near Sachuest Beach, thunders impressively when a sea is running. Historic Portsmouth lies to the north.

8 NARRAGANSETT

Of interest in and around this popular summer resort: The Towers, designed by Stanford White; Scarborough and Sand Hill Cove state beaches; the fishing villages of Galilee and Jerusalem; Point

Judith's Coast Guard Station, open to visitors. At the Narragansett campus of the University of Rhode Island is the Graduate School of Oceanography, the deep-ocean research vessel *Trident*, and the first state-owned nuclear reactor. The Northeast Shellfish Sanitation Research Center is also situated here.

9 NEWPORT

Newport, long considered the Queen of Resorts, has many of the opulent mansions built by the Four Hundred during the Gilded Age prior to and just after World War I. And there are two other Newports to see, as well: Colonial Newport and Navy Newport. The ferry from Jamestown (a summer resort on Conanicut Island, boasting a picturesque old windmill built in 1787) offers a glimpse of Navy Newport before it docks at Ferry Landing, south of Long Wharf: the granite Naval War College building on the left; old Fort Adams on the right. Downtown Newport is Colonial Newport, and among the exceptional number of buildings worth seeing are Wanton-Lyman-Hazard House (1675), the city's oldest house; the Friends Meeting House (1699); Trinity Church (1726), which closely resembles Boston's Old North; Touro Synagogue (1763), second oldest synagogue in the U.S.; Old Colony House (1739), a historically important building; Redwood Library (1748), oldest continuously used library building in America; Hunter House (1748); the Brick Market (1762), designed by Peter Harrison; Vernon House, the Comte de Rochambeau's headquarters during the Revolution; White Horse Tavern (1673). The Newport Historical Society building houses the lovely interior of the Seventh Day Baptist Church (1729). The Old Stone Mill, of controversial origin, stands in Touro Park. Out on Bellevue Avenue and Ochre Point are the fabulous summer homes of the wealthy, a large number of which were designed by the architect Richard Morris Hunt: Cornelius Vanderbilt's The Breakers (1895), and The Breakers stables (on Coggeshall Avenue); E. J. Berwind's The Elms (1901); William K. Vanderbilt's Marble House (1889–92); Oliver H. P. Belmont's Belcourt Castle (1893). These are open to the public. Many of the others can be seen by taking the Cliff Walk or by driving around Ocean Drive, past exclusive Bailey's Beach. Newport is also famous for sailing (America's Cup and Bermuda races), and tennis (Newport Casino Invitation Tennis Tournament and the National Tennis Hall of Fame).

10 PROVIDENCE

State capital of Rhode Island, Providence was founded and named by Roger Williams in 1636. The First Baptist Church (1775) is the meetinghouse for the oldest Baptist congregation in the United States, originally established in 1639. Two other interesting churches are the Beneficent Congregational Church (1809) and the First Unitarian Church (1816). The handsome State House, designed by McKim, Mead and White, overlooks downtown Providence from Capitol Hill. Inside is a famous portrait of George Washington by Gilbert Stuart. The Old State House was built in 1762 (the tower and a wing were added in 1851). Brown University, chartered in 1764, has some interesting buildings: University Hall (1770); John Hay Library; John Carter Brown Library, housing one of the best collections of Americana in the country; Annmary Brown Memorial. Also worth visiting: the elegant John Brown House (1786), home of the Rhode Island Historical Society; the Rhode Island School of Design's Museum of Art; Governor Stephen Hopkins House (c. 1743); Providence Athenaeum (1838); Shakespeare's Head, with its Colonial garden; Carrington House (1812); Betsy Williams Cottage (1773), in Roger Williams Park; Clemence-Goddard-Irons House (c. 1680), in suburban Johnston. In adjoining Pawtucket: Old Slater Mill (1793), the country's first successful textile mill.

11 WESTERLY

The state's westernmost town and shopping center for a string of shore resorts to the south, including fashionable Watch Hill, with its venerable carrousel. Burlingame State Park, to the east in Charlestown, offers swimming, picnicking, and overnight camping. To the north, in Ashaway, is the interesting Tomaquag Valley Indian Memorial Museum.

12 WICKFORD

A charming Narragansett Bay village in North Kingstown, with a great many well-preserved 18th-century houses. The fine Old Narragansett Church (St. Paul's), was built in 1707 and is New England's oldest Episcopal church. In the environs: South County Museum, with Colonial farm tools; Smith's Castle (c. 1679) at Cocumscussoc, possibly the only house standing in which Roger Williams preached; Quonset Point Naval Air Station; the Gilbert Stuart birthplace, where the great portrait artist was born in 1755; and the Samuel Casey Farm (c. 1750).

A statue of Unitarian scholar William E. Channing is near the Old Stone Mill in Newport's Touro Park.

SAMUEL CHAMBERLAIN

CHANNING

For further information write to:
Rhode Island Development Council
Publicity and Recreation Division
Roger Williams Building
Providence, Rhode Island 02908

INFORMATION ROUNDUP: RHODE ISLAND

U.S.	Rhode Island
AMERICA DISCOVERED **1492**	
	1502 CORTE-REAL visits coast
	1524 VERRAZANO explores area
	1614 BLOCK enters Narragansett Bay
PLYMOUTH settled **1620**	
BAY COLONY settled **1630**	
	1634 BLACKSTONE settles at Cumberland
	1636 WILLIAMS founds Providence
	1638 PORTSMOUTH founded
	1639 NEWPORT founded
	1643 WARWICK settled
	1644 CHARTER procured
	1647 UNITED GOVERNMENT formed
	1663 NEW CHARTER granted
KING PHILIP'S WAR begins **1675**	GREAT SWAMP FIGHT
STAMP ACT passed **1765**	
	1769 *LIBERTY* sunk
	1772 *GASPEE* set afire
INDEPENDENCE declared **1776**	INDEPENDENCE declared by Colony
	1793 TEXTILE MILL built by Slater
WAR OF 1812 begins **1812**	
	1815 GALE causes Providence flood
	1842 CONSTITUTION adopted
CIVIL WAR begins **1861**	
	1869 NAVAL TORPEDO STATION established
	1884 NAVAL WAR COLLEGE founded at Newport
SPANISH-AMERICAN WAR **1898**	
	1922 TEXTILE STRIKE
STOCK MARKET CRASH **1929**	
	1938 TIDAL WAVE floods large area
	1940 QUONSET POINT AIR Station begun
U.S. ENTERS WORLD WAR II **1941**	
	1944 HURRICANE strikes state
	1954 TWO HURRICANES strike state
	1955 HURRICANE causes bad flooding
	1960 HURRICANE sweeps across state

TOPOGRAPHY: East (Narragansett Basin), shallow, flat lowlands surrounding Narragansett Bay, which extends 30 miles inland and has an irregular shoreline with many small bays; within the bay are three large islands and numerous small ones; west (New England Uplands), hilly, many small lakes; south, barrier beaches, salt marshes, and lagoons. Altitudes: high, 812 ft.; low, sea level; approx. mean, 200 ft.

MAIN RIVERS: Blackstone, Branch, Pawcatuck, Pawtuxet, Providence, Queen, Seekonk, Wood, Woonasquatucket

LARGEST LAKES: Flat River, Scituate, Watchaug Pond, Wordens Pond

CLIMATE: Cold winters and warm summers; extremely changeable weather; snowfall considerable in west; occasional hurricanes and tidal waves. *Av. temps.*: Providence, July max., 80.0° F; Feb. min., 20.4° F. *Av. ann. precipitation*: Providence, 39.63 in. (snow and sleet, 33.0 in. mean total)

MAJOR CITIES: (1960 census): Providence (207,498); Pawtucket (81,001); Warwick (68,504); Cranston (66,766); Woonsocket (47,080); Newport (47,049)

NATIONAL HISTORIC SITE: Touro Synagogue

STATE PARKS (1960): Arcadia, Beach Pond, Burlingame, Casimir Pulaski Memorial, Dawley, Diamond Hill, Dyerville, Fort Greene, Goddard Memorial, Haines Memorial, Lincoln Woods, Meshanticut, Peter Randall, Seekonk River, Squantum Woods, Ten Mile River; Edmund J. Fay and John T. Owens memorial fields; 4 reservations; 6 historic sites; 3 monuments; 7 beaches; 4 parkways; 29 roadside picnic groves

UNIVERSITIES AND COLLEGES: (Universities) Brown; Rhode Island; (Colleges) Barrington; Bryant; Catholic Teachers; Pembroke; Providence; Rhode Island; Rhode Island School of Design; Salve Regina; U.S. Naval War College

NICKNAME: Little Rhody

MOTTO: Hope

ORIGIN OF NAME: After the Isle of Rhodes in the Mediterranean Sea

AREA (1960): 1,214 sq. mi. (water, 156 sq. mi.); *rank*, 50

POPULATION (1960 census): 859,488; *rank*, 39

CAPITAL: Providence

DATE U.S. CONSTITUTION RATIFIED: May 29, 1790; *rank*, 13

FINANCE (Fiscal 1962): Revenue, $174,246,000
Expenditure, $174,984,000

U.S. REPRESENTATIVES: 2

STATE FLOWER: Violet

STATE TREE: Maple

STATE BIRD: Rhode Island Red

STATE SONG: "Rhode Island" by T. Clarke Brown

THUMBNAIL HISTORY

Narragansett Bay and the coastal waters of Rhode Island were visited by Miguel Corte-Real in 1502, Giovanni da Verrazano in 1524, and Adriaen Block in 1614, and a clergyman, William Blackstone, made his home at present Cumberland in 1634. The first real settlement, though, was founded by Roger Williams at Providence in 1636. Two more colonies were planted at Portsmouth and Newport in 1638 and 1639, respectively, and in 1643 a fourth was established at Warwick by Samuel Gorton. A charter for the first three towns was procured in 1644, and in 1647 all four united under a single government. In 1663 Charles II granted the Colony a new charter guaranteeing comparative religious liberty. During King Philip's War (1675–76) the decisive Great Swamp Fight was fought at North Kingston on December 19, 1675. The Colony's extensive maritime commerce based on the slave trade made it a determined opponent of British mercantilist policies. Newporters burned the revenue ship *Gaspee* in June, 1772, and Rhode Island on May 4, 1776, became the first Colony to declare its independence, but it was not until a rebellion led by Thomas Wilson Dorr broke out in 1842 that a constitution was adopted. After the construction of the first power spinning frame by Samuel Slater in 1790, the textile industry rapidly developed and came to dominate the state's economy. Immigration swelled the population, and ethnic antagonisms were exploited by employers to hinder the effective organization of unions and the passage of social legislation. The flight of textile firms to the South beginning in the 1920's inaugurated a decline in the industry, which was hastened by the depression of the 1930's, but the increased concentration of naval facilities in the state during World War II helped Rhode Island begin to restore its economy. Severe damage was caused by a hurricane and tidal wave in 1938, and the state was again struck by hurricanes in 1944, 1954, 1955, and 1960.

GOVERNMENT and POLITICS

Top state executives and members of the bicameral legislature serve two-year terms. Vote in Presidential elections 1900–1964: Dem., 9; Rep., 8.

ECONOMY

Water—both rivers and the sea—is Rhode Island's single most important natural resource. Because of the abundant water power afforded by the state's rivers, the manufacture of textiles (Rhode Island's leading industry) developed in the early 19th century, and metalworking, from which the present machinery and jewelry industries grew, got an early start. One of the principal employers in the state, though, is the sprawling Newport Naval Base, and a major source of income is summertime tourism at Rhode Island's many seaside resorts. Although much less important than in Colonial times, shipbuilding, especially the construction of pleasure craft, has expanded during the past decade. Commercial fishing has also declined since the 19th century, but an estimated 68,787,000 pounds of fish, with a value of about $4,064,000, were caught in 1963. Farming accounted for only .3 per cent of personal income in 1962.

TRANSPORTATION AND COMMUNICATION (1962)
RAILROADS: 159 line miles
ROADS: 4,380 miles (317 miles nonsurfaced)
MOTOR VEHICLES REGISTERED: 358,960
AIRPORTS (as of Jan. 1): 13 (8 general)
RADIO STATIONS: 15 AM, 6 FM
TELEVISION STATIONS: 2
DAILY NEWSPAPERS (1963): 7

TIMBER (1958)
STUMPAGE CUT: 700,000 cu. ft.
VALUE OF STUMPAGE CUT: Under $500,000

MINERALS: (1962)
VALUE OF MINERALS EXTRACTED: $2,994,000
PRINCIPAL COMMODITIES: Sand and gravel, stone, gem stones

RHODE ISLAND AND U.S. PERSONAL INCOME (1962)
By major sources as per cent of total
U.S. TOTAL: $439,661,000,000
RHODE ISLAND TOTAL: $2,052,000,000

■ RHODE ISLAND ■ U.S.

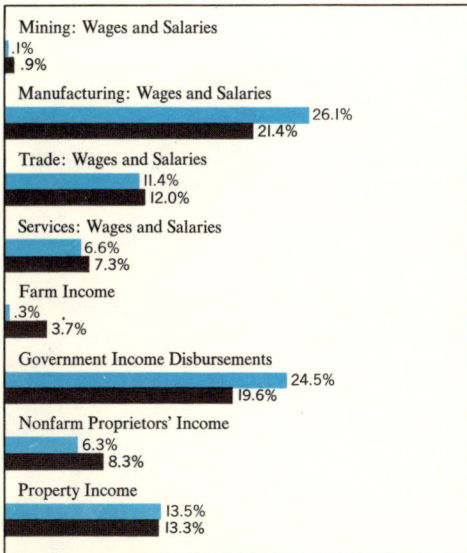

Mining: Wages and Salaries
.1%
.9%

Manufacturing: Wages and Salaries
26.1%
21.4%

Trade: Wages and Salaries
11.4%
12.0%

Services: Wages and Salaries
6.6%
7.3%

Farm Income
.3%
3.7%

Government Income Disbursements
24.5%
19.6%

Nonfarm Proprietors' Income
6.3%
8.3%

Property Income
13.5%
13.3%

PRINCIPAL MANUFACTURES (1962 est.)

Industry	Employees	Value Added* ($1,000)
Textile mill products	24,528	225,303
Machinery, except electrical	10,335	100,396
Rubber and plastics products	9,178	102,202
Primary metal industries	9,314	90,621
Fabricated metal products	8,097	62,399
Food and kindred products	6,110	54,786
Electrical machinery	6,741	52,249
Apparel and related products	4,327	23,759
Instruments and related products	3,239	22,571
Chemicals and allied products	2,105	18,588
Leather and leather products	1,875	15,090
Miscellaneous manufacturing	21,105	147,552

*Value added by manufacture, adjusted

AGRICULTURE (1963 est.)

Product	Harvested Acres	Quantity (1,000)	Value ($1,000)
Potatoes	5,100	1,262 cwt.	2,779
Hay	20,000	35 tons	1,452
Vegetables for fresh market	1,530	142 cwt.	681
Apples	—	150 bu.	360
Peaches	—	13 bu.	52
Cattle & calves (1962)	—	3,580 lbs.	568
Hogs (1962)	—	2,367 lbs.	395
Sheep & lambs (1962)	—	162 lbs.	28
Dairy products (1962)	—	—	6,820*
Poultry & eggs (1962)	—	—	4,600*

*Gross farm income

FISHING (1961)

Species	Catch (1,000 lbs.)	Value ($1,000)
Clams	2,739	1,008
Flounders	5,386	490
Northern lobsters	680	367
Scup, or porgy	7,105	345
Butterfish	2,947	252
Menhaden	22,636	193
Whiting	5,021	124
Cod	1,066	69

TOTAL VALUE ADDED BY MANUFACTURE, ADJUSTED (1962 est.): $1,137,660,000
TOTAL CASH RECEIPTS FROM FARMING (1962 est.): $20,480,000
TOTAL VALUE OF FISH CATCH (1962): $3,528,000

SOUTH CAROLINA

For many decades after the Civil War the impoverished aristocrats of South Carolina lulled themselves with dreamy reminiscences of the glorious epoch in which the state led the South and played a decisive role in the affairs of the nation. Little was left to them but their memories. The plantations had become dusty patchworks of tenant farms, the once robust cotton plants were shriveling, and the future seemed bleak and hopeless.

But amid pervasive despair there were men with bolder dreams. They established textile mills, and as these succeeded, the lassitude that had set in throughout the state began to be dispelled. Gradually, South Carolinians straightened their backs. A new epoch, with more hope for the future than the old one, dawned.

South Carolina today is undergoing a great reconstruction. Industry and commerce are expanding at a faster rate than in most other states. The farms, though still poor, are being revitalized through soil conservation and diversification—though cotton (opposite) is still a leading crop. Consequently, the standard of living, which has been among the lowest in the country, is being raised, and relative prosperity has come to the state.

However, South Carolina remains rooted in custom. In some cases, this has been the cause of great travail; in others, traditions have taken on new meaning.

AN ARISTOCRATIC PAST

The Cypress Gardens were once a rice reservoir.

EUGENE B. AND KATHLEEN LEWIS SLOAN

Before the eight lordly proprietors of Carolina dispatched the first boatload of settlers to their colony in 1670, they procured from the English philosopher John Locke a constitution, which ordained for the wilderness settlement a rigid social structure headed by a noble class of landgraves, caciques, and barons. The constitution was abandoned in 1693 —barely 23 years after the founding of Charleston—and with it went, although not immediately, the inappropriate titles. But the tone and affectations of aristocracy were harvested in as great abundance as were the crops of rice, indigo, and, later, cotton, which were the chief sources of the planters' wealth.

The criteria of social status were the amount of land and number of slaves a man owned, particularly the latter, and even a merchant might acquire the aristocratic appellation of "planter" by buying enough slaves and some land, whether or not he continued to engage in trade. This was a parvenu aristocracy, numbering among its most distinguished members people who had made their start in life as weavers, hostelers, tradesmen, and artisans. Blood was of little account in Colonial South Carolina.

Despite their mean beginnings, or perhaps because of it, the planters were particularly assiduous in imitating the panache and levity of British high society. In the 18th and early 19th centuries Charleston was a little London. Each spring, traditionally on May 10, the plantation owners and their families would flee the malaria-ridden marshes of the low-lying regions for their mansions in the capital, and the season of balls, musicales, and theatrical entertainments would last until crisp autumn weather made the country habitable again. But the aristocrats were no less attentive to the accouterments of good breeding. A comparatively literate group, they corresponded with European intellectuals, imitated the best English architecture (for example, St. Michael's Church is in the style of James Gibbs's St. Martin's-in-the-Fields), and sent their sons to Oxford and Cambridge. As the dour New Englander Josiah Quincy remarked in 1773, "state, magnificence, and ostentation, the natural attendants of riches, are conspicuous among this people: the number and subjection of their slaves tend this way."

The Civil War shattered the economic foundations of the aristocracy, but the planter class, though largely dispossessed and impoverished, became all the more tenacious of its traditions. To this day, South Carolina's first families constitute an exclusive and highly self-conscious society. The Ravenels, Manigaults, St. Simons (their name is now Simons), the Pinckneys, Balls, Bulls, Rhetts, and Middletons enjoy almost as much prestige in South Carolina as the peers of England were once afforded by the commoners of their country. A member of one of these families who marries outside this class is said to have "married down," and offspring of the union are considered more or less *déclassé*. The St. Cecilia Society, a musical organization founded in 1762, is still in existence, and to the balls it holds every year in the stately Hibernian Society Hall, only the social elite are invited; the *nouveau riche* are disdainfully excluded. (The *nouveau riche*, though—the textile mill executives and other successful businessmen—have themselves adopted certain aristocratic ways, such as donning formal attire for dinner.)

"Charleston," John Gunther wrote, "is a gem; it is also a kind of mummy." The city is a vast museum, in that respect something like Florence, Italy. Just walking down the older streets one sees some of the finest architecture in America. On Rutledge Avenue is the mansion of Pat-

rick Duncan, now the Ashley Hall school for girls. Dating from about 1816, the house, with its slender columns, graceful curves (especially the elliptical staircase), and elaborate woodwork, is the quintessence of the elegance and ease so esteemed by the magnates of the period. The Miles Brewton (Pringle) House on King Street, which is considered to be among the most distinguished examples of the Georgian-style home on this continent, reflects the hardiness and simplicity of the successful merchant for whom it was built in 1765. Just outside the city is Middleton Place, whose formal gardens, completed in 1741 after 10 years' work by 100 slaves, are a lovely, if rather extravagant, expression of Charleston's predilection for things English. Most of these old mansions are presently inhabited, in some instances by descendants of their builders.

Charleston's Cabbage Row (below, left) was the prototype for the Catfish Row setting of George Gershwin's opera Porgy and Bess. *Rainbow Row's multihued houses (right) brighten the water front.*

Fishermen crowd the pier at Myrtle Beach, the most popular resort center of the Grand Strand.

THE COMMERCIAL RENAISSANCE

Even while dallying at their pastimes, the shrewd merchant-planters of Charleston kept a sharp eye out for what was happening at the water front. Through the busy port passed most of South Carolina's exports, which just before the Revolution accounted for about 40 per cent of the goods shipped to England from all the Colonies. In the early 19th century Charleston, along with New Orleans and Mobile, conducted most of the South's thriving export trade in cotton. But after the Civil War the port became relatively insignificant.

Since the establishment of the South Carolina State Ports Authority in 1942, Charleston has once again become an important funnel for the nation's foreign commerce. By 1950 it had taken away from Northern ports the bulk of the import trade in long-staple cotton, thereby saving the South Carolina textile mills as much as $7 a bale in rail freight costs, and by 1962 it had become the country's leading inlet for foreign wool. In 1962 Charleston handled $283,700,000 worth of imports and exports, thus ranking fourteenth among all United States seaports in the value of the foreign commerce passing through their facilities. Georgetown, about 50 miles to the north, has developed a substantial business in the shipment of lumber and, since 1962, in the importation of oil. And with the dredging of the harbor at Port Royal, that tiny town of 686 people also began to emerge as an artery for coastal and foreign trade.

The development of these long-dormant ports has had a far-reaching effect on

South Carolina's economy. It is estimated that one third of the new industry established in the state since 1945 is attributable to the expansion of the port facilities. For example, as a result of the increased importation of wool, which as recently as 1953 was virtually nil, about $60 million has been invested in plants that process and scour wool during the last 10 years. Agriculture has benefited by the greater access to distant markets. About $2 million more income a year is received by the farmers of South Carolina because the construction of a new grain elevator at Charleston Harbor has enabled them to store and ship corn inexpensively.

Another major factor in South Carolina's commercial renaissance has been the concerted promotion of tourism by the state and by private interests. In 1962 out-of-state tourist expenditures amounted to $130 million, an increase of about 175 per cent since 1948. The most popular resorts are along "the Grand Strand," a 50-mile strip of sandy beaches and gentle surf warmed by the Gulf Stream, which flows only about 40 miles offshore. At the center of the Grand Strand is Myrtle Beach, a year-round vacation spot offering everything from deep-sea fishing for bass, sting ray, and sand shark, to surf bathing and carnivals. Other nearby ocean front communities include Crescent Beach and Brookgreen.

Farther down the coast are the Sea Islands, long famous throughout the world for their flourishing plantations until an infestation of boll weevils in the early 1920's destroyed the excellent long-fiber cotton. Hilton Head Island, with its languid South Seas atmosphere, has become increasingly popular since the erection of a toll bridge from the mainland in 1956. For vacationers seeking the clear air and seclusion of the mountains, there is the Blue Ridge chain in the west, although facilities for out-of-town tourists are not yet extensive in this area.

EUGENE B. AND KATHLEEN LEWIS SLOAN

The palmetto is a common tree along the coast.

Charleston Evening Post

The port of Charleston has become a major trade artery. Below, newsprint is shipped out.

SOUTH CAROLINA STATE DEVELOPMENT BOARD

STRUGGLING AGRICULTURE

About 350,000 bales of cotton were shipped from Charleston in 1860. Mechanical pickers (below) are now used on the larger cotton farms.

Rarely did the New World bestow its bounty so ungrudgingly as it did on the early settlers of South Carolina. The inland and coastal swamps proved admirable for cultivating rice, and by 1700 a substantial export trade in the grain had already developed. Then in 1744, after three years of patient experimenting, Elizabeth Pinckney, nee Lucas, induced the loamy soil of her father's plantation near Charleston to bring forth a crop of indigo, which was in great demand by the rapidly expanding English textile industry for the blue dye produced from its leaves. Some cotton was also raised, although very little was shipped abroad.

But it was cotton that ultimately emerged as the greatest money-maker. In 1801 the state legislature authorized the expenditure of $50,000 for one of Eli Whitney's cotton gins. This remarkable machine for separating the seed from raw cotton drastically reduced the cost of processing and thus stimulated a rapid expansion of production. South Carolina's output shot up from 50,000 bales in 1801 to 350,000 bales in 1860. Ultimately, however, cotton was South Carolina's undoing. Improper cultivation ruined the soil in many areas. The failure to diversify (indigo cultivation had virtually disappeared after the American Revolution and rice was the only other major crop), as well as the lack of industry, made the state's economy excessively dependent on the unstable Northern and English markets for cotton. And, worst of all, as the margin of profit thinned due to the greatly increased production, the use of slave labor became all the more necessary.

The disastrous effects are being felt to this day. When the slaves were freed, South Carolina was impoverished. A feudal-like system of farm tenancy and

Tobacco, now the state's main crop, is strung in preparation for curing in this fieldside barn.

sharecropping developed, and since most of these farmers were penniless, they borrowed, putting up their future harvests as collateral. Without slave labor, rice cultivation was unprofitable and dwindled to virtually nothing, which left cotton as the only cash crop. Production increased for a while, but this forced prices even lower, throwing the farmers more deeply into debt. In an attempt to save themselves, they tried to grow more cotton on the same land and thus further exhausted the soil. By the end of the 19th century the plight of the South Carolina farmers was desperate.

The situation is still poor. In 1959, 30.8 per cent of the farms were operated by tenants, as compared to 19.8 per cent for the United States. The average value per farm of land and buildings was $15,685, and the average value per farm of agricultural products sold was only $3,933, while the averages for the United States were $34,826 and $8,232, respectively. Only about 35 per cent of South Carolina farms

had telephones, which is just a little more than half the average for the United States as a whole.

There has been notable improvement, however. Diversification has been proceeding steadily. Cotton no longer accounts for two thirds of farm income, as it did in the 1920's, but only for about one fifth. Tobacco is now the leading crop, and only California surpasses South Carolina in the value of the annual peach harvest. Between 1950 and 1962 the number of beef cattle and calves on farms rose threefold, and commercial broiler production increased 177 per cent. There has been considerable mechanization and consolidation of farms, which in the case of South Carolina has had a salutary effect by taking marginal land out of cultivation. Extensive soil conservation measures, such as the planting of soybeans, have been taken. But the state has a long way to go before the agricultural prosperity of the period before the Civil War will be restored.

Orlon, a synthetic fiber, is made at Camden.

E. I. DU PONT DE NEMOURS AND COMPANY

Undyed textiles, "gray goods," are inspected.

A broken strand of denier nylon yarn is mended.

At a factory in Clemson, women sew hems and put other final touches on sheets manufactured there.

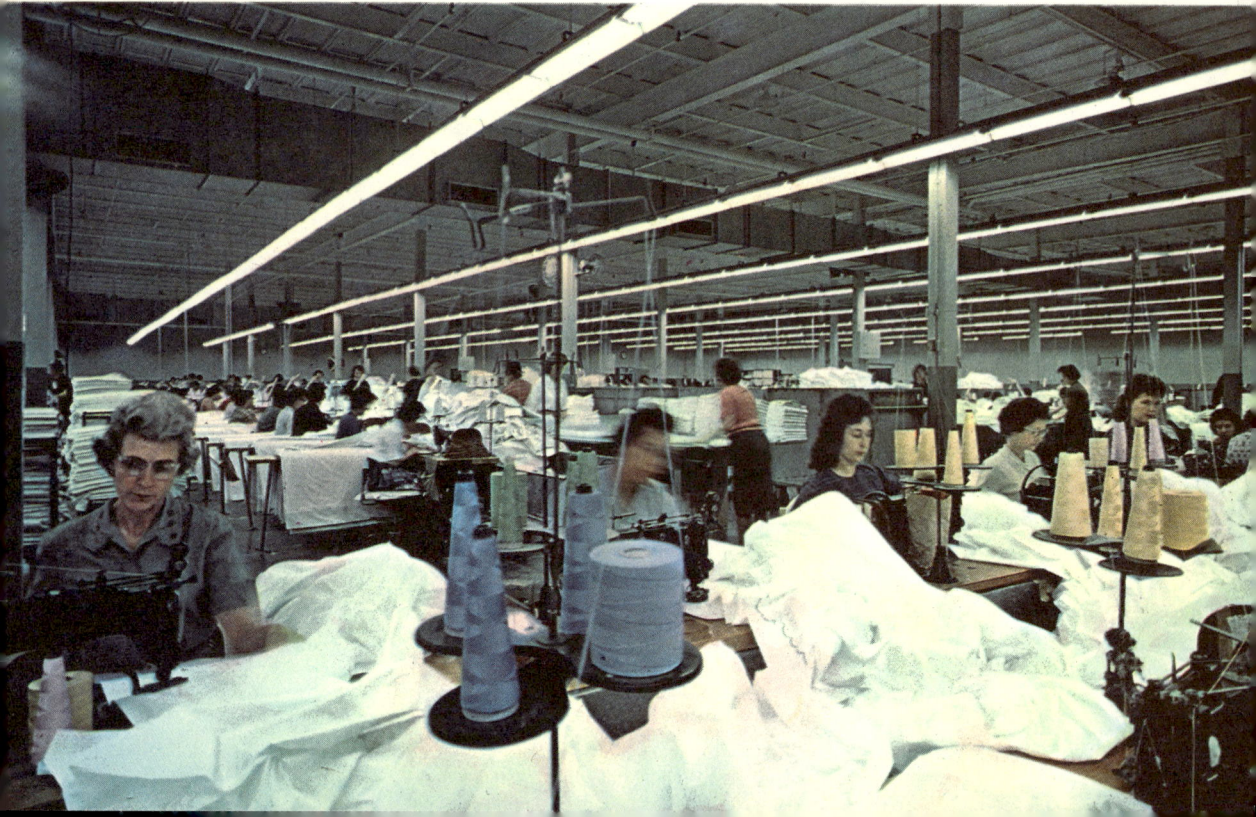

GOLDEN SPINNING WHEELS

The folly of not developing local industry was brought home to South Carolina when the Congress in 1828 enacted a tariff on imports, which threatened to have the effect of reducing English purchases of raw cotton because of the reduced sale of English manufactured goods in the U.S. For five years controversy raged between Northern interests favoring protection and the Southern planters, who were led by South Carolina's John C. Calhoun. A compromise was worked out in 1833, and the bitter sectional antagonisms that were to bring about the Civil War were temporarily mollified. But South Carolina was in no position to rectify the basic economic problem. Too little capital was available, most of it having been sunk in land and slaves. Moreover, aristocratic notions about the contemptibleness of trade discouraged planters from investing in manufacturing.

Due to the efforts of William Gregg, who established a large cotton mill at Graniteville in 1846, and a handful of other foresighted men, at least a beginning of industrialization was made. By 1860 there were 17 mills, employing 891 operatives, in the state. The Civil War interrupted this development, but in 1870 the Reconstruction legislature, in which a large number of freedmen served, stimulated renewed expansion by granting the mills exemption from taxation for four years. A factory containing no less than 10,000 spindles was set up in 1876, and by 1900 there were 115 mills in operation. Most of these located in the Piedmont because of the availability of cheap labor in the area and the abundance of streams for water power.

There are now about 340 textile plants in South Carolina, and in terms of the market value of the textile products manufactured—$2.4 billion in the year ending mid-1962—the state is surpassed only by North Carolina. Cotton goods are, of course, the staple of the industry, but in recent years synthetic fabrics, such as plastic and glass-fiber yarns and rayon and nylon tire cord, have become increasingly important, as have woolens.

Expansion is continuing at a prodigious rate. In 1963 alone $93 million was invested in new factories and equipment—on top of $200 million in similar investments during the preceding four years. But, paradoxically, this has actually had the effect of reducing employment, because a substantial amount of the money has been put into automated machinery. There are now about 6,000 fewer production workers in the industry than there were a decade ago. Automation has also forced out of business many of the old, family-owned textile mills that could not afford the expensive equipment necessary to reduce costs to a competitive level.

One of the major reasons for this expansion has been the removal to South Carolina of Northern textile firms, which are attracted particularly by the effective resistance to unionization in the state. Only about 10 per cent of the textile workers belong to trade unions, as compared, for example, to 37 per cent in New York and 61 per cent in New Jersey. In 1954 the legislature enacted a right-to-work law prohibiting labor-management agreements that require workers to join a union as a condition of employment. Although wage rates in the industry are only slightly lower than the national average, other benefits ordinarily provided for in union contracts, such as seniority rights and effective grievance machinery, are often lacking. The loss of jobs due to automation, however, has given new impetus to organizational activities in South Carolina by the unions.

ENTERING THE NUCLEAR AGE

Wood chips are cooked in "digesters" until they form pulp for manufacturing paper and board.

Just as the agriculture of South Carolina was based for a long time on a single crop, cotton, so its industry for many years was limited almost exclusively to the manufacture of cotton into yarn and cloth. Since the market for textiles is extremely mercurial, surging and declining in response to general economic fluctuations, irregularities in the weather, fickle tastes in fashions, and a variety of other factors, South Carolina's economy was very unsteady.

In conjunction with the state's efforts to achieve stability in the agricultural sector of the economy through diversification, a program for attracting new and varied industries was instituted in the 1940's. Probably the most important step, in terms of long-range effects, was the revitalization of the Port of Charleston beginning in 1942. Three years later a state development board was established,

and various tax advantages have been provided, such as elimination of the state property tax, exemption of production machinery and repair parts from the retail sales tax, and a *no situs* law that permits goods in transit from one state to another to be assembled, stored, or processed in South Carolina without being subject to an impost on inventories. In 1961 the legislature established the State Committee for Technical Education to provide training for workers in new and more sophisticated job skills.

Largely as a result of this program, $1,655,000,000 was invested between 1950 and 1962 in the construction of 630 new manufacturing plants and the expansion of 835 old ones. Much of the growth, of course, has been of industries that are directly or indirectly related to textiles. For example, 80 new apparel factories went into operation during those 12 years alone, and since the early 1950's, chemical manufacturing has developed into a major industry because of the greatly increased

Blue granite is cut from Winnsboro quarries.

A chair base is made at a new furniture plant.

production of synthetic fibers by the state's textile firms. But there has also been a notable expansion of industries that exploit South Carolina's 12 million acres of softwood and hardwood forests. From the loblolly, shortleaf, and other varieties of pine, $210,560,000 worth of pulp and paper were ground out in 1962 by 23 pulp and paper mills (21 more than were in existence at the end of World War II). The number of furniture and woodwork plants increased from a mere 20 in 1945 to 144 in 1962.

In at least one field South Carolina has been an important innovator. The first electrical plant in the Southeast to use nuclear power, and one of the first in the nation, was completed at Parr Shoals near Columbia in 1963. Four power companies —one of which, the South Carolina Electric and Gas Company, is a local concern —formed a corporation to build the plant in co-operation with the Atomic Energy Commission, which supplied funds for research and technical assistance. The heavy water used in the nuclear reaction is manufactured at the Savannah River Plant, a large installation near Aiken for the proc-

essing of fissionable materials. Established in 1952, the Savannah River Plant is run by E. I. du Pont de Nemours and Company for the AEC.

Gradually, South Carolina is pulling itself out of the chronic economic depression in which it has languished virtually since the end of the Civil War. It is estimated that 116,000 new jobs were created during the period from 1950 to 1962 by industrial expansion and that total payrolls increased by about $280 million a year. Per capita income, though still the lowest in the country except for Mississippi and Arkansas and well below the national average, rose from $882 in 1950 to $1,545 in 1962. With this has come a marked improvement in the standard of living. In 1960, 60.7 per cent of the housing units in the state had adequate plumbing facilities, as compared to 34.3 per cent in 1950, and there have been significant increases in the percentage of homes with refrigerators, telephones, radios, and the other amenities of modern life. There is still a long way to go before South Carolina will catch up with the rest of the United States, but progress is being made.

The state has a program for training labor.

SOUTH CAROLINA FLORA AND FAUNA

BIRDS

1) Wood Ibis; 2) Glossy Ibis;
3) Willet; 4) American Oyster Catcher;
5) Carolina Wren

TREES

1) Cabbage Palmetto; 2) Blackjack Oak;
3) Sourwood; 4) American Holly

FLOWERS

1) Spatterdock; 2) Spiderwort;
3) Carolina Jessamine; 4) Tillandsia

ANIMAL LIFE

1) Alligator; 2) Rainbow Snake;
3) Bullfrog; 4) Marsh Rabbit

HARRY MCNAUGHT

VANGUARD OF THE SOUTH

On a hot night in mid-June, 1822, a group of Negroes met secretly at the Charleston home of Denmark Vesey, a former slave who had bought his freedom, and made final plans for a slave uprising scheduled for later in the month. They were betrayed, and Vesey, along with 34 other men, was hanged, but the conspiracy had shattered white complacency.

The struggle to maintain slavery, and thus prevent the ruin of the plantation economy, became an increasingly nightmarish preoccupation of the state's leaders. Threatened both by the slaves themselves, who constituted the majority of the population, and by the rising abolitionist sentiment throughout the country, South Carolina became the vanguard of the South in maneuvering to preserve the institution. As enunciated by the state's most brilliant spokesman, Senator John C. Calhoun, the arguments for slavery were elevated to a defense of the doctrine of states' rights. The U.S. Constitution, he insisted, was a compact of sovereign powers, and "the two governments, State and Federal, must of necessity be equal in their respective spheres." Therefore, the Federal Government had no right to interfere with slavery. On December 20,

John C. Calhoun

Dilapidated shacks are still the homes of many Negroes.

1860, South Carolina put the doctrine to the test by becoming the first state to secede from the Union; on April 12, 1861, Rebel troops at Charleston fired on Fort Sumter to begin the Civil War.

Although the war resulted in the freeing of the slaves and the preservation of the Union, states' rights has remained a burning issue to this day, and the system of racial segregation that was made mandatory by a series of Jim Crow laws passed in the 1890's is still by and large maintained. As of November, 1963, only 10 Negro children were enrolled in white schools. The state parks were closed in 1960 to prevent their being used by Negroes, and when they were reopened in 1964 the swimming facilities and cabins remained shut. However, there is growing concern among whites that racial tension might hinder economic development. At his inauguration in 1963, Governor Donald S. Russell made a significant gesture by inviting Negroes to a lawn party. In that same year Negro students were admitted to Clemson University and the University of South Carolina without incident. It is expected that as a result of the Civil Rights Act of 1964 barriers to integration will drop more quickly.

The firing on Fort Sumter began the Civil War.

School integration has proceeded very slowly.

SOUTH CAROLINA LEGENDS AND LORE

During the Revolution a young British officer was led, blindfolded, into the American camp. When the cloth was taken from his eyes, he stared at the unshaven men in homespun and leather—a sharp contrast to the Tory officers with their elegant uniforms. In front of him stood the dreaded Swamp Fox, General Francis Marion, whose hit-and-run raids on the English and loyalist troops from his base in the South Carolina marshes had made his name a terror among His Majesty's forces. Marion stepped forward and the negotiations for an exchange of prisoners began. After the details were settled, dinner was served. "Sweet potatoes smoking from the ashes were placed upon a piece of bark and set before the general and his guest." Astonished at such penury, the redcoat inquired:

"Doubtless this is an accidental meal; you live better in general?"

"No, we often fare much worse," Marion replied blandly.

"Then I hope you draw noble pay to compensate?"

"Not a cent, sir, not a cent."

The bewildered officer gulped down his "wine," consisting of vinegar and water, and, so the story goes, upon returning to British headquarters at Georgetown promptly resigned his commission and left for England. "What chance have we against such men?" he reasoned.

The fire and stubbornness of the South Carolina militia was—and, indeed, is—particularly characteristic of the Up Country farmers, such as "the stiff-necked Scotch-Irishman" who earnestly used to pray: "Lord, grant that I may always be right. For thou knowest that I am hard to turn."

South Carolina's women demonstrate the same peppery quality no less than the men. One of the first voices in America for women's rights was raised in 1734 by a Carolina belle who wrote in the *South Carolina Gazette*:

Then equal Laws let Custom find,
And neither Sex oppress:
More Freedom give to Womankind
Or to Mankind give less.

This poetical polemic was answered in kind by an anonymous gentleman:

JOHN ALCORN

Dear Miss, of Custom you complain:
It seems to me you languish,
For some dear, simple, homely Swain
To ease you of your Anguish.

The state's most striking native folk tales are to be found among some of the Sea Island and coastal Negroes, who speak a strange dialect called Gullah, which is probably derived from the mingling of English with a tongue brought from Western Africa. "Po' buckruh an' dog walk one pat'" (the poor man and the dog walk the same path). Animals were favorite subjects in the Gullah tales. Buh Hawss and Buh Mule were turned out together in the pasture one Sunday when "the high buckruh" was away. Buh Hawss, who pulled the fancy carriage of the buckruh, pranced around the pasture, switching his fine tail to keep the flies off his hindquarters. He looked at the sparse little tail of Buh Mule, and "Buh Hawss biggin fuh brag. 'Look 'puntop oonuh tail,' 'e say. 'Oonuh yent kin switch fly 'long um 'cause 'e shabe. Shishu no'count tail ent wut." ("Buh Hawss began to brag. 'Look, at the top of your tail,' he say.

'You can't switch the flies way up there 'cause it's shaved. What a no-account tail.'") Ashamed, Buh Mule hung his head and walked over to the other side of the pasture to think. Suddenly he began to laugh. Buh Hawss ambled over to find out what was so funny. Buh Mule pointed to the cornfield beyond the fence and laughed. "Buh Hawss ent smaa't 'nuf fuh jump de fence en' run'um uh race t'ru de cawnfiel'." "Buh Hawss tek 'um up." He jumped the fence, knocking over the rails, and started to gallop through the corn. Buh Mule trotted after him. As they raced through the field, Buh Hawss's silky tail "biggin fuh hebby" from the sheep burrs clinging to it, while none stuck to Buh Mule's scrawny little tail. The horse switched his tail back and forth, but succeeded only in getting it more entangled with the burrs, which stung his haunches each time he tried to thrash them off. "'E say to 'esulf, 'wuh dis t'ing? Me fuh lick me own self! Me fuh hab spuhr een me own tail!'" Just then Buh Mule trotted by, and, contemplating Buh Hawss's tail, mused gratefully about his own: "Tengk Gawd fuh shabe tail!"

Table Rock Mountain, seen rising above Table Rock Reservoir, is a peak of the Blue Ridge chain.

Waterfalls, cascades, and rapids mark the Fall Line.

Motorboats along the Congaree River

UP COUNTRY AND LOW COUNTRY

Running diagonally from northeast to southwest down the middle of South Carolina is a long, narrow strip of land characterized in many places by waterfalls and river rapids. The Fall Line, as it is known, marks where the Piedmont highlands drop suddenly to the Atlantic coastal plain. But it is more than a division point between two geographic sections. Between "the Up Country" and "the Low Country" are major historical and cultural differences.

The Low Country was, until the Civil War, the undisputed dominion of the plantation-owning nabobs, the greatest proportion of whom were English or French in origin and distinctly English in taste. They controlled South Carolina even after the Up Country people wrested

more equitable representation in the legislature from the Tidewater aristocrats after the American Revolution. In his speech the Low Country man softens his *r*'s and lets the syllables of his words glide lightly one to the other. Whether poor or rich, he cherishes the traditions of South Carolina society.

The Up Country, which includes the Blue Ridge Mountains area, as well as the Piedmont Plateau, was settled later, mostly by Scotch-Irish and Germans, who carved small farms for themselves out of the wilderness and owned few slaves. A fiery group, these backwoodsmen tended to be much more democratic, if somewhat less refined, than the inhabitants of the Low Country. The characteristic twang in their speech is still discernible.

When the textile industry took root in the Piedmont area after the Civil War, economic and political control of South Carolina passed to the Up Country. Greenville, which calls itself the Textile Center of the World—not without some justification—grew into the second largest city in the state. It is trying now to woo new industries, and a number of concerns that make chemicals, machinery, and metal products have located there. Spartanburg, about 15 miles east of Greenville, has also become an important industrial city, and the surrounding country, once a blighted region of impoverished cotton farms, is extensively planted in prospering peach orchards. Both cities have become cultural centers. Furman and Bob Jones universities are located in Greenville, and Spartanburg has three colleges. The future economic growth of the Up Country, however, is closely tied to the successful redevelopment of the ports of the Low Country, and this mutual dependency is helping to bind the two sections more closely together.

1071

THE ENDURING COMPROMISE

During the furious debates that raged between the inhabitants of the Low Country and the Up Country after the Revolution, at least one source of contention was removed by an agreement to transfer the capital of South Carolina from Charleston to Columbia. Situated in the very center of the state, just below the Fall Line, the city would belong exclusively to neither section and thus, it was hoped, would help promote an enduring spirit of compromise.

As Columbia grew, it took on characteristics of both regions—the industriousness and comparative democracy of the Up Country; the sense of gracious living and love of culture of the Low Country. It became the commercial center of the state, which it still is today. There are tall modern buildings housing the commercial firms and government agencies that are the major employers in the city, and there are factories making such products as metal goods, lumber, Fiberglas, fertilizer, plastics, and, of course, textiles. But Columbia is also the home of the University of South Carolina, founded in 1801, and four other schools of higher education. The State House, construction of which was begun in 1855, is one of the most elegant capitols in the United States. Unfortunately, only a few of the luxurious ante bellum mansions survive because most of the city was put to the torch by General Sherman in 1865. However, the classical De Bruhl–Marshall House, dating from 1820, and the white-frame Guignard House, which was built around 1800, indicate how the tastes of the planter aristocracy were applied to the more modest dwellings of the Columbians. The latter home, incidentally, escaped burning due to the efforts of a slave cook, who, after her masters had fled, sought out Sherman and offered him the best cooking in all of Columbia, a tempting offer that resulted in the Union officers' setting up their headquarters in the house.

In other cities where the attributes of the two sections mingle there is often a feeling of incongruity. Aiken, for example, is renowned not only for the AEC Savannah River Plant nearby, but also for its polo matches, fox hunts, and other equestrian pastimes of the aristocracy. At Camden, where horse lovers gather every spring for the Carolina Cup Steeplechase and to canter along the 200 miles of bridle paths, there are textile mills and a number of other factories. Darlington is a quiet Southern small town situated in one of the state's most fertile cotton and tobacco growing districts, but it also has the second largest automobile speedway in the United States.

As a rule, one characteristic or the other tends ultimately to prevail. Sumter in pre-Civil War days was the gathering place for the aristocracy from neighboring plantations and developed into a cultural center. It even had an opera house, at which performances were given by traveling companies. The city is now a principal furniture-making center, although a vestige of its past remains in the Swan Lake Iris Gardens. On the other hand, the towns and villages around Lakes Marion and Moultrie, where many of the aristocrats used to spend their holidays, are still predominantly resorts. They are especially popular with fishermen, because the lakes are well stocked with striped bass, bluegill, and crappies.

In general, however, the spirit of compromise has endured throughout South Carolina. It typifies the modern development of the state. The Low Country dedication to tradition perseveres amid the growing preoccupation with economic progress and democracy.

Columbia (top) was laid out in a checkerboard pattern to help prevent the spread of malaria. The Southern 500 stock car race (bottom) is a Labor Day event at Darlington. Jousting tournaments are held at Kingstree (center left). The Avenue of the Oaks plantation (center right) was used in the filming of Gone with the Wind.

SOUTH CAROLINA PLACES OF INTEREST

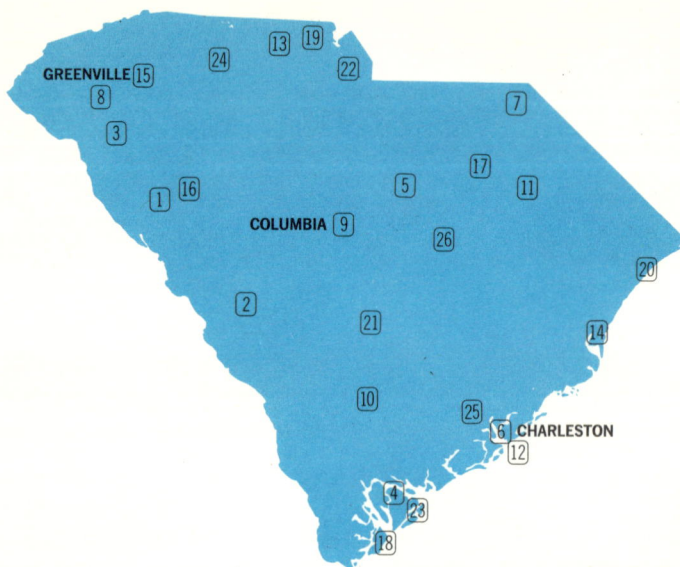

1 ABBEVILLE
The Confederate Cabinet met for the last time at Burt Mansion on May 2, 1865.

2 AIKEN
Polo matches have been held at this popular year-round resort for 75 years, and there are also fox hunts, drag hunts, and flat racing. Nearby is the Atomic Energy Commission's Savannah River Plant for the manufacture of fissionable materials.

3 ANDERSON
Founded in 1826, this town was named for General Robert Anderson, a hero of the Revolutionary War. Near Anderson, which is only an hour's drive from the Blue Ridge Mountains, are a number of lakes with good recreational facilities.

4 BEAUFORT
The second oldest town in the state (1711), Beaufort is the site of short-lived 16th-century colonies founded by the French and Spanish. It was devastated by Indians in 1715, captured by the British in the Revolution, and held by Union forces during the Civil War. Despite its turbulent history, which also includes the ravishments of two hurricanes, this romantic town on Port Royal Island has a number of well-preserved ante bellum houses standing along oak-shaded streets. Among the many points of interest are the National Military Cemetery, where 12,000 Union soldiers are buried along with a small group of Confederates; St. Helena's Episcopal Church, built in 1724; the ruins of Sheldon Church, which was built in 1745–57, partially destroyed by the British during the Revolution, rebuilt, and

burned again by Sherman's troops; Beaufort Arsenal (constructed in 1795 with crushed oyster shells), housing two British trophy guns seized in 1799; the Crofut House, a brick building built in the 1850's. Beaufort's picturesque harbor, with its many shrimp boats, is the scene of yearly yacht regattas. On nearby Parris Island is a monument to the first French Huguenot settlers and a large Marine training center. Also in the vicinity are Port Royal, the site of Fort Frederick; and Hunting Island State Park, a beach resort with facilities for camping and fishing.

5 CAMDEN
Steeplechase races are run here on one of the most difficult courses in the nation, and there are many horse shows, polo games, flat races, and fox hunts during the tourist season, which lasts from January to April. The Bethesda Presbyterian Church, designed in Greek Revival style by Robert Mills in 1820, and the Quaker Cemetery are of interest. The first of a projected annual parade and Revolutionary War battle re-enactment was held in Camden in November, 1964.

6 CHARLESTON
This splendid city is famous for its beautiful Colonial houses with their verandas and ironwork balconies; narrow cobblestone streets; and a wide variety of historic buildings and landmarks, as well as beaches, gardens, and plantations. Settled in 1670, Charles Town, as it was then called, was the capital of South Carolina until 1786. It is now the third largest city in the state and one of the chief seaports in the Southeast. Among the many historic sights are

the Georgian St. Philip's Episcopal Church (1838), the graveyard of which is the burial place of John C. Calhoun and other distinguished South Carolinians (during the Civil War this church displayed a mariner's light in its lofty steeple to guide blockade runners and was a target for bombardment by Union troops); St. Michael's Church, begun in 1752, with chimes that have been transported across the Atlantic five times; the Dock Street Theatre, the first building in America designed as a playhouse, twice burned and rebuilt according to the original model, and still in continuous use; the Old Powder Magazine, part of the city's original fortifications, now a historical museum; the French Huguenot Church (1845), said to be the only church in the country adhering to the exact form of Huguenot worship; Rainbow Row, a group of typical 18th-century houses along the water front, so-called because each house is painted a different color; the Old Slave Mart Museum and Gallery; Charleston Museum (1773), one of the oldest museums in the nation, featuring early South Carolina crafts, furniture, and other relics; the Gibbes Art Gallery, which includes works by South Carolina artists; the City Hall, built in 1802, containing many priceless portraits, the best known of which is John Trumbull's painting of George Washington; the Heyward-Washington House (1770); the early Georgian brick home of Thomas Heyward, Jr., signer of the Declaration of Independence; the Nathaniel Russell House (c. 1809), a fine example of post-Colonial architecture, with exquisite interior paneling; the Thomas Legare House (1760), which features a Regency piazza and contains many pieces of old furniture and portraits; the Miles Brewton (Pringle) House (c. 1769), a typical Georgian "double house," enclosed with a handsome iron fence; the Joseph Manigault House. Tours of these and other historic homes in Charleston are conducted in the spring by the Historic Foundation. Forts Sumter and Moultrie are located

Ruins of twice-destroyed Sheldon Church, Beaufort

in the city's harbor. In or near Charleston are several public and private gardens. Middleton Place, which has one of the oldest landscaped gardens in America, was built about 1755 by Henry Middleton, president of the Continental Congress; gingko trees, giant live oaks, azaleas, camellias, and magnolias form a vivid array of colors along the rolling terraces. At the tropical Cypress Gardens, 250 acres of three-century-old cypress trees, azaleas, magnolias, and daffodils grow along the black waters of a former rice reservoir. On the banks of the Ashley River are internationally famous gardens, including azaleas, magnolias, wisteria, rare trees, and over 500 varieties of camellias. Also of interest: Hampton Park, a picturesque spot with a zoo, sunken gardens, and landscaped lawns; Avenue of the Oaks (Boone Hall) Plantation in nearby Mount Pleasant, with its original slave quarters, a cotton ginning house, formal gardens, and restored mansion approached through a romantic avenue of live oaks, used as a setting for the movie *Gone with the Wind*. Just northeast of Charleston is the Francis Marion National Forest, which has 245,000 acres of scenic areas abounding with moss-draped live oaks, old plantations, recreational sites, fishing streams, and good hunting areas; it also contains the Indian Mound Archaeological Area and the adjoining Cape Romain National Wildlife Refuge, a large bird sanctuary. Significant educational institutions in the Charleston area include the College of Charleston, which was founded in 1785, and the Citadel, a state military college with a fine historical museum.

7 CHERAW

In the graveyard of St. David's Episcopal Church (1770–73) are interred British soldiers who died of smallpox in the Revolution. The church had been temporarily converted into a hospital during an epidemic.

Cheraw's historic St. David's Church and graveyard

8 CLEMSON

Fort Hill, a beautiful old mansion on the campus of Clemson University, was the home of John C. Calhoun and his son-in-law Thomas G. Clemson and contains many of the original furnishings. Nearby is the Old Stone Church, a fine example of pioneer workmanship; it is the burial place of General Andrew Pickens.

9 COLUMBIA

The state capital and largest city, Columbia was almost entirely rebuilt after General Sherman set fire to it the night of February 17, 1865. The imposing Italian Renaissance State Capitol, begun in 1851, is one of the few buildings that survived the conflagration; on the landscaped grounds are several monuments and memorials. The Columbia Museum of Art and Science has the state's largest exhibition of art and includes the priceless Kress Collection of Renaissance paintings, as well as Spanish colonial artifacts, sculpture, ceramics, and furniture; in the science section are natural history exhibits and a planetarium. The Archives Building preserves important historical manuscripts and has a Confederate relic room, where sabers, uniforms, flags, and other articles pertaining to the Confederate era are displayed. The house in which Woodrow Wilson lived for a while during his childhood has been turned into a museum and contains mementos of the President's career. The South Carolinian Library, on the campus of the University of South Carolina, is the oldest separate college library in the nation and houses manuscripts and relics relating to the state's history. The First Baptist Church is where the Secession Convention met in December, 1860. Among the few remaining ante bellum homes are the De Bruhl-Marshall House, a Greek Revival mansion, and the Guignard House. In the vicinity of Columbia are the ruins of Millwood, which was burned by Sherman's troops; the boyhood home of General Wade Hampton; Lake Murray, formed by the Saluda Dam; and Fort Jackson, a large U.S. Army post.

Fort Hill, the Calhoun home on the Clemson campus

SOUTH CAROLINA STATE DEVELOPMENT BOARD

EUGENE B. AND KATHLEEN LEWIS SLOAN

The University of South Carolina Library, Columbia

10 EHRHARDT

Rivers Bridge Memorial State Park marks the site of the Salkehatchie River crossing, where outnumbered Confederate forces held Sherman's troops in check for two days, winning a successful delaying action.

11 FLORENCE

Nearby fishing areas and beautiful flower gardens attract visitors to this industrial town. Of interest are the site of the Civil War Stockade, and National Military Cemetery, where Union soldiers who died in prison are buried; the Florence Museum, with exhibits of American Indian art, regional history, and crafts from other counties.

12 FORT SUMTER NATIONAL MONUMENT

The national monument includes Fort Sumter, located on a small sand bar in Charleston Harbor, and Fort Moultrie on Sullivan's Island. Fort Sumter was the scene of the bombardment by Confederate troops on April 12, 1861, that started the Civil War. Seized by Confederate troops, it was under heavy attack for 20 months by Union forces. The Confederacy did not evacuate it until February 17, 1865. The fort has been recently restored and includes gunrooms, barracks, and markers. Guided tours are available. Fort Moultrie, which is presently being restored, was the scene of Revolutionary War battles and is the burial place of Osceola, the Seminole Indian chief; it was also the setting for Edgar Allen Poe's story "The Gold Bug."

13 GAFFNEY

Just north of here is the Cowpens National Battlefield Site, scene of a brilliant American victory by General Daniel Morgan over a superior British force, January 17, 1781.

14 GEORGETOWN

Near this seaport are Brookgreen Gardens, a showplace with majestic moss-hung live oaks (some of the oldest in North America), lily ponds, a wildlife refuge, and a zoo. In the gardens, which were the setting for Julia Peterkin's novel, *Scarlet Sister Mary*, is a large collection of American sculpture. Also nearby: Belle Isle Gardens, the birthplace of General Francis Marion, containing the ruins of an old Civil War fort and informal gardens with brilliant azaleas, camellias, and oaks; Hampton Plantation, a Georgian mansion dating from 1735, which is the home of Archibald Rutledge, the state's poet laureate.

15 GREENVILLE
Of special interest in this large textile center situated on the rolling Piedmont Plateau are the Greenville Museum and the art and Bible collection of Bob Jones University. Resorts in the vicinity include Caesars Head, a mountain resort since ante bellum times; Table Rock State Park; and Paris Mountain State Park.

16 GREENWOOD
Nearby is the site of Ninety Six, the oldest white settlement in western South Carolina. The pioneers named the city for the safe distance between them and the Indian village of Keowee. Earthen remains of a British stronghold, Star Fort, can also be seen. For recreation, Greenwood State Park and Sumter National Forest afford good fishing for trout and bass and hunting for deer, turkey, and quail.

17 HARTSVILLE
Kalmia Gardens, a lush arboretum, has over 700 varieties of trees and shrubs intermingled with azaleas and other flora.

18 HILTON HEAD ISLAND
One of the Sea Islands, this is a popular year-round resort. In the summer there are swimming, fishing, boating, and a variety of other sports. From October to March the island affords excellent bird hunting.

19 KINGS MOUNTAIN NATIONAL MILITARY PARK
This is the site of a battle on October 7, 1790, in which frontiersmen defeated British troops. Among the monuments near the center of the battlefield is the U.S. Government Obelisk, authorized by Congress in 1909. There is also a museum. A nearby state park has scenic nature trails and campsites.

20 MYRTLE BEACH
The state's largest and most popular seaside resort has miles of sparkling beach and white sand dunes, with extensive facilities for water sports, golfing, and fishing. A state park is nearby.

21 ORANGEBURG
The beautiful Edisto Memorial Gardens, located on the banks of the Edisto River, consist of approximately 60 acres of azaleas, moss-draped trees, and camellia-japonicas; there are also a Japanese iris garden, a Chinese water wheel, and a test garden of the American Rose Society, as well as tennis courts, swimming areas, a playground, and picnic facilities.

22 ROCK HILL
The children's Nature Museum in this textile center has exhibits of wildlife, as well as of African and Indian artifacts. Nearby is the Andrew Jackson His-

The ante bellum Capitol survived Sherman's torches.

torical State Park, site of Jackson's birthplace, where there is a museum containing mementos and documents associated with the Indian-fighting President. A pioneer village, a lake, and recreational facilities are also being developed at the park.

23 ST. HELENA
One of the largest of the Sea Islands, St. Helena was discovered by Spanish explorers in the 16th century. The town is chiefly populated by the Gullah-Negroes, who still retain many of the customs of their African ancestors and speak a unique dialect. Frogmore and other ante bellum plantations are in the vicinity.

24 SPARTANBURG
A few miles from Spartanburg is Foster's Tavern (1812), which was an overnight stopping place in the early 19th century for travelers between Georgia, North Carolina, and Virginia.

25 SUMMERVILLE
South of here is the Old Dorchester State Park, located on the site of a town established by New England Puritans. In the park are the tower of the Anglican Church of Saint George, and the remains of an old fort dating from about 1757.

26 SUMTER
Australian swans swim amid the cypress, flaming wisteria, and Japanese iris of the Swan Lake Iris Gardens. A few miles from Sumter is Dundell Gardens, the former estate of General Thomas Sumter, which has a large lake surrounded by iris, azaleas, and dogwood.

> *For further information write to:*
> *Travel and Information*
> *State Development Board*
> *Columbia, South Carolina 29202*

INFORMATION ROUNDUP: SOUTH CAROLINA

U.S.		South Carolina
AMERICA DISCOVERED	**1492**	
	1521	SLAVING EXPEDITION by Quexos, Cordillo
	1526	WINYAH BAY COLONY established
	1562	PORT ROYAL COLONY founded
ST. AUGUSTINE founded	**1565**	
	1566	SPANISH settle at Parris Island
JAMESTOWN settled	**1607**	
	1629	CHARLES I grants area to Heath
	1663	CHARLES II gives charter to proprietors
BRITISH take New Amsterdam	**1664**	
	1670	CHARLESTON founded
	1729	ROYAL COLONY status given by king
	1744	FIRST INDIGO harvested
	1761	CHEROKEE INDIANS defeated
AMERICAN REVOLUTION begins	**1775**	PROVINCIAL CONGRESS meets
	1780	BRITISH capture Charleston
	1786	COLUMBIA becomes capital
COTTON GIN invented	**1793**	
	1801	COTTON GIN bought by state
WAR of 1812 begins	**1812**	
	1822	VESEY SLAVE CONSPIRACY quelled
JACKSON elected President	**1828**	
TARIFF of 1832 passed	**1832**	NULLIFICATION law passed
COMPROMISE of 1850	**1850**	
	1860	SECESSION
CIVIL WAR begins	**1861**	FORT SUMTER fired upon
	1865	COLUMBIA burned
RECONSTRUCTION ends	**1877**	TROOPS withdrawn
U.S. ENTERS WORLD WAR I	**1917**	
	1921	BOLL WEEVIL plague begins
U.S. ENTERS WORLD WAR II	**1941**	
	1942	PORTS AUTHORITY established
WORLD WAR II ends	**1945**	DEVELOPMENT BOARD set up
SCHOOL INTEGRATION ordered	**1954**	
	1960	STATE PARKS closed
	1963	NUCLEAR POWER PLANT completed
CIVIL RIGHTS ACT passed	**1964**	PARKS reopen with limited facilities

TOPOGRAPHY: East and south, the Atlantic Coastal Plain (the Low Country), flat along the coast and gently rolling inland; northwest (the Up Country), uplands with rolling hills in the Piedmont Plateau section, leading into the Blue Ridge Mountains along the northwestern border. Altitudes: high, 3,560 ft.; low, sea level; approx. mean, 350 ft.

MAIN RIVERS: Broad, Combahee, Congaree, Edisto, Lynches, Pee Dee, Saluda, Santee, Savannah, Wateree

LARGEST LAKES: Catawba, Clark Hill, Greenwood, Marion, Moultrie, Murray, Wateree Pond

PRINCIPAL MOUNTAINS: Blue Ridge Mts. (Sassafras Mtn., 3,560 ft.; Pinnacle Mtn., 3,413 ft.; Hogback Mtn., 3,226 ft.; Caesars Head, 3,218 ft.)

CLIMATE: Hot and humid summers; mild winters, but with occasional cold spells; temperatures vary according to latitude, elevation, and distance from the ocean. *Av. temps.*: Columbia, July max., 91.9° F; Dec. min., 35.8° F. *Av. ann. precipitation*: Columbia, 46.15 in. (snow and sleet, 1.8 in. mean total)

MAJOR CITIES (1960 census): Columbia (97,433); Greenville (66,188); Charleston (65,925); Spartanburg (44,352); Anderson (41,316)

NATIONAL FORESTS: Francis Marion, Sumter

NATIONAL PARKS: Kings Mountain National Military Park; Cowpens National Battlefield Site

NATIONAL MONUMENT: Fort Sumter

STATE PARKS (1960): 22 (largest: Cheraw, Croft, Kings Mountain, Hunting Island); Fort Watson, General Thomas Sumter, and Eutaw Springs state historical sites; Colleton State Wayside

UNIVERSITIES AND COLLEGES: (Universities) Bob Jones; Clemson; Medical College of South Carolina; South Carolina; (Colleges) Allen University; Benedict; Charleston; Claflin; Coker; Columbia; Columbia Bible; Converse; Erskine; Furman University; Lander; Limestone; Lutheran Theological Southern Seminary; Morris; Newberry; Presbyterian; South Carolina State; The Citadel; Winthrop; Wofford

NICKNAME: Palmetto State

MOTTO: *Animis Opibusque Parati* (Prepared in spirit and resources); *Dum Spiro Spero* (While I breathe, I hope)

ORIGIN OF NAME: For Charles I of England

AREA (1960): 31,055 sq. mi. (water, 783 sq. mi.); *rank*, 40

POPULATION (1960 census): 2,382,594; *rank*, 26

CAPITAL: Columbia

DATE U.S. CONSTITUTION RATIFIED: May 23, 1788; *rank*, 8

FINANCE (Fiscal 1962): Revenue, $399,005,000
Expenditure, $365,390,000

U.S. REPRESENTATIVES: 6

STATE FLOWER: Carolina Jessamine

STATE TREE: Cabbage Palmetto

STATE BIRD: Carolina Wren

STATE SONG: "Carolina" by Henry Timrod and Anne Custis Burgess

THUMBNAIL HISTORY

Following a slaving expedition to the South Carolina coast by Pedro de Quexos and Francisco Cordillo in 1521, the Spanish in 1526 planted a settlement at Winyah Bay, only to abandon it a few months later. A French colony founded in 1562 at Port Royal (present Beaufort) and another Spanish settlement established in 1566 at Parris Island also failed to survive. In 1629 Charles I of England bestowed the region upon Sir Robert Heath, but the unexploited grant was passed on by Charles II in 1663 to a group of eight proprietors, under whose auspices a colony was founded in 1670 on the Ashley River. Rice and indigo plantations worked by slaves came to dominate the Low Country, and after South Carolina became a crown colony in 1729, settlement of the Up Country was promoted. The defeat of the Cherokee Indians in 1761 opened the way for more extensive settlement of the Piedmont by small farmers, whose antagonism toward the tidewater planters was slightly mitigated when the purchase by the state of a cotton gin in 1801 made cotton growing profitable to both sections. To protect its cotton trade, South Carolina declared the Tariff of 1832 nullified, and largely to maintain slavery, the state led the South into the Civil War by being the first to secede from the Union (December 20, 1860) and by ordering its militia to fire on Fort Sumter April 12, 1861. The refusal of the state legislature to ratify the Fourteenth Amendment brought military occupation, which was not withdrawn until 1877. After the war, the plantation system was displaced by farm tenancy and sharecropping, and Jim Crow laws passed in the 1890's and a new constitution adopted in 1895 made racial segregation mandatory. An economic renewal has been taking place since the 1940's, but there is apprehension that racial tensions, marked by the closing of most state parks in 1960 to avoid integration, might impede further development.

GOVERNMENT and POLITICS

The governor and state senators have four-year terms; state representatives serve for two years. Vote in Presidential elections 1900–1964: Dem., 15; Rep., 1; States' Rights, 1.

ECONOMY

Although there have been considerable agricultural diversification and industrial development in South Carolina during the past two decades, cotton is still the staple of the economy. The state's principal industry, the manufacture of textiles, is based largely on cotton produced by local farmers, and even though tobacco is now the leading crop in terms of market value, cotton lint and seed together rank a close second. Lumbering and the furniture and paper and pulp industries are becoming increasingly important. Except for granite and limited amounts of vermiculite and barite, minerals of significant commercial value have not been found in South Carolina. Commerce has been expanding rapidly as a consequence of the revival of the Port of Charleston. Per capita income in 1962 was only $1,545, the third lowest amount in the U.S.

TRANSPORTATION AND COMMUNICATION (1962)
RAILROADS: 3,266 line miles
ROADS: 57,085 miles (23,504 miles nonsurfaced)
MOTOR VEHICLES REGISTERED: 936,601
AIRPORTS (as of Jan. 1): 78 (35 general)
RADIO STATIONS: 88 AM, 15 FM
TELEVISION STATIONS: 10
DAILY NEWSPAPERS (1963): 17

TIMBER (1958)
STUMPAGE CUT: 352,500,000 cu. ft.
VALUE OF STUMPAGE CUT: $35,850,000

FISHING (1963 est.)
CATCH: 22,010,000 lbs.
VALUE OF CATCH: $3,236,000
PRINCIPAL SPECIES: Shrimp, oysters, mullet, spot, blue crabs, sea bass

SOUTH CAROLINA AND U.S. PERSONAL INCOME (1962)
By major sources as per cent of total
U.S. TOTAL: $439,661,000,000
SOUTH CAROLINA TOTAL: $3,763,000,000

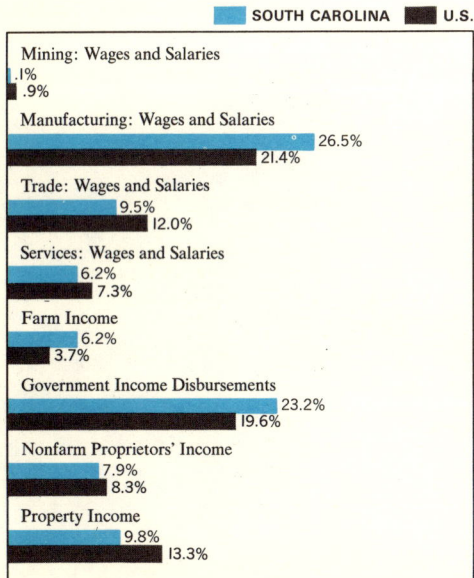

■ SOUTH CAROLINA   ■ U.S.

Mining: Wages and Salaries
.1%
.9%

Manufacturing: Wages and Salaries
26.5%
21.4%

Trade: Wages and Salaries
9.5%
12.0%

Services: Wages and Salaries
6.2%
7.3%

Farm Income
6.2%
3.7%

Government Income Disbursements
23.2%
19.6%

Nonfarm Proprietors' Income
7.9%
8.3%

Property Income
9.8%
13.3%

AGRICULTURE (1963 est.)

Product	Harvested Acres	Quantity (1,000)	Value ($1,000)
Tobacco	80,000	168,000 lbs.	100,800
Cotton lint	537,000	455 bales	75,530
Soybeans for beans	710,000	12,070 bu.	33,192
Corn for grain	526,000	22,618 bu.	29,403
Peaches	—	7,700 bu.	20,020
Hay	332,000	386 tons	12,159
Vegetables & melons for fresh market	61,700	3,439 cwt.	12,069
Cotton seed	—	189 tons	9,091
Oats	175,000	5,600 bu.	4,480
Wheat	70,000	1,890 bu.	3,496
Sweet potatoes	8,500	552 cwt.	2,318
Pecans	—	10,000 lbs.	2,130
Peanuts, picked and threshed	11,000	13,200 lbs.	1,597
Cattle & calves (1962)	—	123,770 lbs.	23,303
Hogs (1962)	—	124,655 lbs.	20,568
Dairy products (1962)	—	—	31,008*
Poultry & eggs (1962)	—	—	48,200*

*Gross farm income

PRINCIPAL MANUFACTURES (1962 est.)

Industry	Employees	Value Added* ($1,000)
Textile mill products	129,466	923,630
Chemicals and allied products	17,438	348,446
Apparel and related products	34,349	133,579
Paper and allied products	7,799	91,329
Food and kindred products	10,289	90,126
Stone, clay, and glass products	6,994	71,418
Lumber and wood products	15,614	67,011
Electrical machinery	4,761	39,933
Furniture and fixtures	3,053	21,069
Tobacco products	1,143	7,556

*Value added by manufacture, adjusted

PRINCIPAL MINERALS EXTRACTED (1962 est.)

Product	Quantity (1,000 short tons)	Value ($1,000)
Stone	6,382	10,066
Clay	1,518	7,165
Sand and gravel	3,318	3,670
Items that cannot be disclosed	—	13,000

TOTAL VALUE ADDED BY MANUFACTURE, ADJUSTED (1962 est.): $1,976,809,000
TOTAL CASH RECEIPTS FROM FARMING (1962 est.): $428,587,000
TOTAL VALUE OF MINERALS EXTRACTED (1962 est.): $33,901,000